COURAGEOUS

FIRE

COURAGEOUS AND PASSIONATE LEADERSHIP

TERRENCE DAVIS

Thoughts on Courageous Leadership

"Courageous leaders lead with passion. They take the time to dream, feel passionate about their dreams, and infuse that passion into the hearts and minds of the people they lead. This is a key element of courageous leadership as it has been true in my own experiences supporting other leaders."

~ Roni Habib, speaker, author, and founder of EQ Schools

"Fear is part of the human condition, we all face fear. The goal is not let fear paralyze you as a leader. As leaders, inaction is a silent killer. Be Courageous! Have an opinion and make decisions, this is what we signed up for. It is better to make the wrong decision, than to make no decision at all."

~ Michael R. McCormick, Retired Superintendent, AVID Resident Superintendent

"Courageous leadership is about creating the conditions for your team to be able to say the hard things out loud, embrace failing forward, and always "go first" to model that WE really means WE."

~ Janice Case, West Regional Director, National Center on Education and the Economy

"Courageous leadership is about boldly embracing innovation and creating conditions that champion equity and excellence, even when it's challenging."

~ Jerry Almendarez, Superintendent and Futurist

"Courageous leadership is not about the absence of fear in times of challenge, but instead it is the resolve to stand for what is right and just, even in the middle of the storm."

**~ Dr. Gordon Amerson,
Superintendent and Education Thought Leader**

"Inspiring innovative practices to ensure access for all students requires leaders to lead with courage, be bold, and challenge the status quo. In order for leaders to move the needle for our most vulnerable students, it requires courageous leadership."

~ Leah Davis, Riverside County SELPA Director

"Courageous leadership in the TK-12 environment requires individuals to prioritize the best interests of their students over adult conveniences."

~ Dr. Adam Clark, Superintendent

"Courageous Leadership is a creed characterized by altruism and selflessness that is sustained by pure vulnerability. In short, it is a calling."

~ Dr. Tonia Causey-Bush, Education and Instructional Expert

"Courageous leadership is about being vulnerable, willing to call things and people in (not out) and navigate teams on to new spaces knowing your own inadequacies will surely be exposed. One person's passion can ignite the fire but fanning the flame is a collective mission, not an individual one. Courageous leaders can take the heat, indeed they thrive in it."

~ Andy Krenz, Director of Regional Sales Strategy

Dedication

This book is dedicated to my parents. My mother, Gloria Lucas-Davis, who I lost this past year, taught me how to be resourceful and fun and care for people in a compassionate manner. My father, Paul E. Davis, built the principles of discipline, integrity, and hard work in me from infancy.

Without their love, direction, and guidance, I would not be the person, father, and leader I am today. The spark was planted a long time ago.

Foreword

Foreword by Dr. Michael T. Conner

CEO/Founder, Agile Evolutionary Group, Corporation.

The era of the AC-Stage of Education (After COVID-19) has presented unprecedented dimensions that make tomorrow unpredictable. More than ever in the history of mankind, leadership has become pivotal to meeting these unknown challenges. It also presents a unique problem: – balancing opportunity and challenge for sustainable impact. We cannot rely on legacy principles to move the pendulum forward at this juncture in our history. Even if that entails taking calculated risks that underpin the need for transformation

It was during the annals of human civilization that visionaries who dared to be courageous enacted authentic progress in their respective verticals. The unapologetic transformists and fearless innovators who were courageous enough to be different when the world told them to be complicit. By definition, it was the need for these individuals to be courageous to address global challenges that have unfortunately become ubiquitous in specific segments of our world. Yes, courageous leadership is the baseline plank to address these intersectional quandaries that many contend will take a seismic effort to redefine standardization.

One might ask to define and articulate the sequential steps of being courageous when the odds are heavily against creating a new normalization for all. Author Terrence Davis unpacks the notion of how to be courageous during uncertain times, albeit there is one resonating theme he presents in his book. Taking action and a critical stance without fear are the first steps in defining courageous leadership during a novel time of uncertainty. This description of courageous leadership outlined by Author Davis goes beyond the trajectory of implementing traditional strategies with making difficult decisions in an organization. Davis highlights in his text that courageous leadership is nuanced and multifaceted. It is a compelling act of vulnerability while having the vision of creating a future that is sustainable despite the noted obstacles of leadership.

In context, courageous leadership cannot be a desirable attribute in this fourth iteration of the Industrial Revolution. As Davis underpins in his book, courageous leadership is an absolute necessity to redefine life outcomes for the future of the world. The courage to change the status quo and root innovation as a precursor for transformation requires the intentionality and boldness to take action. Being courageous, as Davis contends, is stepping outside of your comfort zone and embracing the notion of being comfortably uncomfortable. Davis reminds us that fundamental change in any dimension of leadership or life implicitly challenges our mental model to achieve the desired outcome. In a paradigm where being courageous from a leadership context brings skeptics, Davis provides critical insight on how to be resilient without compromising your values as a leader. Exploring the multiple facets of courageous leadership in the words of Davis will challenge all readers to reassess their current assumptions of courageous acts to manifest a new reality for the future. This text offers a refreshing perspective that provides practical strategies to cultivate courage as a thread in any leader's portfolio. As Peter Senge highlights in his book *The Fifth Discipline*, all readers will experience creative tension with shifting their current mind frame of leadership to desired outcomes of being courageous in a time when it is grossly needed.

The book's content is not another rendition of a text you add to your vast library of literature regarding leadership. Moreover, it is not a text you read to recite theory without action for systemic change. It is a clarion call, a structured blueprint that provides a source of inspiration for leaders who dare to lead in an increasingly complex world. Davis finds a compelling exploration of what it means to be courageous where intersectionality and ambiguity are amplified. As you go through this liberating journey of how to shift your practices and mindset in the context of courageous leadership, you will discover through the work of Author Davis that leadership is not limited to chosen individuals. Rather, courageous leadership is a mental model that can be applied by anyone who wants to embark on a journey of self-discovery and growth. Davis suggests in this text, you will develop your courageous fire to empower and influence the lives in your community.

It is not a secret that we are living in a period where novel outcomes lead to static practices because of the unknowns regarding the future. In essence, Davis describes with depth that it is the perfect time to be courageous as we want courageousness to be contagious for strategic action. Davis inspires us through his text to take an intentional, bold, and unapologetic approach to pursue audacious goals to achieve the impossible.

As a former Superintendent of Schools, there were many decisions where I had to take a courageous stance despite known opposition and pitfalls to prevent progress. I learned that courageous leadership is unpopular because it is fundamentally different from the status quo. Author Davis's text reminded me that it was okay to lead with courage and kindness while developing a heart to forgive. His text also explicitly reminded me that there is a courageous fire in everyone. Thank you, Author Terrance Davis, for outlining the essential principles of courageous leadership in your book. As you stated in the text, the future belongs to those who lead with courage. We are ready to join you to create positive change in our organizations, but more importantly in the world.

Preface

This book highlights pivotal memories throughout my life that have sculpted me into the leader I am today. *Courageous Fire* was created in 2018 in preparation for a presentation at a national conference I was attending. I worked with Andy Krenz on the presentation, and as a result of our several conversations, *Courageous Fire* was created.

The following description is what defines *Courageous Fire*:

"There is no courage in standing over the masses and casting orders like lightning bolts from the mountaintop."

Today's most dynamic leaders serve shoulder to shoulder with the people who impact the lives of students and the people in their community. They embrace the challenge of teaching and learning. They accept the discomfort of vulnerability. They commit to the hard work of meeting each student and person where they are to address what they specifically need. They are willing to not only listen deeply but to respond with grace. "Courage" is defined by such disciplines.

Leaders in education also need something more. They need passion. They need inspiration. They need "fire." So where do they find it? Students, teachers, parents, and community members, like flint to steel, provide the spark. Courage is listening to them. Fire is responding with passion. "Courageous Fire is ACTION!"

I am grateful you are taking the opportunity to hear my story and act upon the steps to strengthen your leadership skills. The more you practice, the stronger you become. #LeadWithCourage #CourageousFire

I would like to thank all of the individuals who have assisted me in the completion of this book. To my wife Leah, two daughters Presli and Kyli, and son Trent: Thank you for providing me with inspiration, material, patience, and balance to complete the work.

Table of Contents

Introduction

"Their greatest fear is that you may step forward without fear. Because your courage may become contagious." ~ Tom Althouse

Have you ever wondered what it means to be courageous?

It's that moment when you know you must take ACTION! You try to curb your nerves and fears, but you take ACTION anyway.

Maybe you've never thought about why you do this or questioned what prompts or pushes you to act, but maybe this is something you should begin to harness.

Ask yourself, what pushes you to take action?

That's your internal spark. It encourages you to take courageous actions, and although part of you feels resistant, your courage motivates and drives you toward the things you want and know are needed. Even though you may feel fear, you drive forward regardless. A leader is a role model to many, so as the initial quote suggests, this courageousness becomes contagious because you inspire others to make their own waves.

In this book, we'll focus on courageous fire, which ultimately refers to that spark that motivates you. If you're wondering how courageous fire enhances leadership, it's all about that passion and motivation you lead with. As a leader, you must also be inspirational, present, and consistently aware of the immediate context. Courageous fire is the flame that ignites your courage muscle and drives you to act. It tells you that it's time to stand up for what you believe in, take risks, and encourage others to do the same.

It's at the heart of a great leader!

A person who leads with courage is a proactive and inspiring role model for others as they demonstrate bravery, determination, and resolve while

1

influencing and guiding the members of their team. They're ready to face challenges head-on, overcoming any obstacle that stands in their way. They have values, and they lead with those in mind, all while keeping the overall vision in mind.

In today's world, courageous leadership is an extremely important quality. Employers want confident, proactive, forward-thinking changemakers in leadership roles who are ready to make a difference, but *how does a leader get there? How do they become courageous? How do they ignite their courageous fire?*

I'll share 'how' as you make your way through this book.

Courage is particularly important when you're in, or aspire to be in, a leadership role. It's a key quality that every modern leader who wants to make a positive difference should develop. That's because it drives and inspires you to:

- Make difficult decisions.

- Make bold moves.

- Take advantage of the opportunities that come your way.

All these things are tasks that a leader must do well regularly if they want to be successful. So, if you want to progress, move forward with momentum, and are ready to gain identifiable results, you need to take courageous action. This book is the first step and will show you how by sharing everything you need to know to ignite your leadership muscle.

Here, I'll help you find your own courageous fire, and I'll share my personal experiences and stories throughout to demonstrate how I found my courageous fire. The journey wasn't always easy, but I learned so many things along the way. We'll explore the idea of courage and its different forms, considering how courage is used in leadership today. We'll unravel the secrets to developing your own inner strength while also learning how to navigate the fear and uncertainty you may face. Fear has a role to play in everybody's life, but here, we'll focus on how you ensure it doesn't prevent you from doing the things you want to do or the things you need to do while also embracing key strategies to help you overcome the barriers in your way. We'll also consider your vulnerabilities and how you can use them for the greater good, and of course, we'll review different ways to confront and overcome fears so you become confident using your courage muscle.

We all need courage to navigate the challenges we face in life, and that's why this book also explores adversity and the different techniques you need to navigate this. It provides you with the opportunity to consider strategies to help you increase your resilience and bounce back from setbacks. This book is about taking positive action, and therefore, you'll also consider courageous acts of kindness and learn to harness the power of kindness and compassion. These things teach us a lot, speak volumes about our character, and provide us with the opportunity to ignite our own courageous fire.

Have you ever had an exceptional, inspiring leader or role model that you looked up to? They had an impact on you, *right?*

The best leaders are dynamic and impactful, and because of that, we remember them. A modern leader of today often must be adaptable, able to challenge ideas, a forward thinker, and willing to step out of their comfort zone when needed. Courage is needed to challenge the status quo and stand up for what is right, and as a leader, this is up to you. That's why we'll be exploring different ways to ignite our courageousness, as this isn't always an easy thing to do, but courageous leadership is a challenge that you must be ready for, and this book will help prepare you for the challenges that lie ahead.

Courage is also important in relationships, and while this book is focused on leadership, it will review both personal and professional relationships and consider the role your courageous fire plays. Self-doubt is typically something that can prevent you from embracing your courage, so we'll explore internal struggles that can get in the way of courageous actions. Ultimately, the more courageously you act, the more your confidence will grow, which is another important leadership quality you need to develop because the most inspiring and courageous leaders radiate confidence.

Another important part of courage is learning to forgive. Forgiveness is often the bravest thing to do, and at times, it can test us. This book will encourage you to question whether you dare to forgive. The act itself is more powerful than most people give it credit for, so you'll also explore strategies to help you understand how finding the courage to forgive and heal positively aids your personal development.

When you've developed your own courageous fire, it's something you should cultivate in others, so this book will also explore ways of cultivating courage in childhood to help you understand its importance. We are shaped by our childhood experiences, and I'm sure that we can all reflect on an event (or several) from our childhood that has made an impact on our lives. You'll explore ways to nurture courage in children and consider the roles parents, educators, and mentors play in fostering courage. It's time to empower the next generation by sharing what you know so that they can harness their courage from a young age. That's because courageous fire is movement!

In the final chapter, we'll provide different strategies and techniques to help you tap into your courageous fire in your everyday life and embrace your courage as a guiding principle.

Throughout this book, you'll explore other successful people who are courageous, both historically and more recently, as their stories are intertwined, to strengthen our understanding of how important courage is. I'll also share a range of personal stories and experiences that helped me shape my own courageous fire that prompted me to break down barriers and become a transformational leader.

There are three key concepts that you will focus on while on this journey to create and cultivate your own authentic, courageous fire. They include:

1. Connectedness

2. Social interaction

3. Community

So, it's important to keep them in mind as you make your way through this book because they matter! Being courageous has been a critical component in all the leadership roles I have been in, and several of my colleagues have shared that I have somehow inspired so many others while on this courageous journey.

My leadership philosophy has always been to leave a place in a much better state than when I found it, and this is something I live and lead by. My courageous fire has helped me do just that, and I truly believe that today's most dynamic leaders are the ones who impact the lives of the people they lead, making a better community, encouraging connectedness, and improving social interactions.

Courageous fire is extremely important because I've always been driven to remain ahead of the game when it comes to changes and challenges in my profession. After earning my Bachelor of Science in criminal justice, I went on to earn a Master of Education in special education and teaching, and I started to understand how education can empower others. I was ultimately responsible for empowering others, and this is a role I've always taken seriously.

I aim to authentically inspire and empower others by sharing my experiences and pushing for change. My expertise is backed by many years of professional experience in education, and I have also established myself in the field as an inspirational speaker over the last twenty-six years.

While my career is filled with highlights, I take the most pride in becoming a pillar of trust and hope for others, and I feel my success stems from the support and guidance of my mentors, who always believed in me. It's always been a goal of mine to drive personal development, improvement, and growth, and I'm lucky enough to have had the support I needed to achieve the things I want to achieve. Now it's my turn to support you!

My own experience has led me to believe that courage and education work together, as they both empower others. I've written this book in light of this so I can help other leaders find their courage, ignite their courageous fire, and impact others for the better. This is exactly why I want to share my courageousness with the world so that you, too, can lead passionately and fearlessly with confidence.

I embraced my courage as I headed into my leadership role and have constantly driven change ever since, even though I've had my fair share of bumps in the road. I don't just drive any change. I drive positive change that I believe in, which is ultimately driven by my courageous actions, and I'll show you how to do this as we progress.

Are you ready to:

- Learn why you should lead with courage and how to do so.

- Develop your courageousness by taking action.

- Reduce the fear you feel as a leader and leap over barriers that stand in your way.

- Stay passionate and motivated and inspire others to be courageous.

- Empower others by cultivating a culture of teamwork, respect, and commitment in the workplace.

You're going to need to keep reading. It's time to find and embrace your courageousness and lead with passion, fearlessly, as you navigate life as a dynamic, modern leader of today.

As we dive deeper into this book, there are a few things I want you to bear in mind. The idea of leadership is constantly evolving, and while there was a time when a person took on a leadership role simply to gain a promotion, a pay rise, and to progress their career, it's no longer that simple. Once you cross over into leadership, it's no longer about you. A recent survey conducted by the Society for Human Resource Management (2023) suggests that 84 percent of US workers who have quit their jobs blamed this on poor leadership, which led to unnecessary stress.

We can change this by developing our skills and leading courageously. As a leader, you are the changemaker, and you're responsible for your team, its performance, and its contribution to the world. You should do this by developing your authentic style that sets you and your team on your courageous journey to success.

Leadership is not about having power or controlling others or situations; it's about empowering and enabling others. Now ask yourself:

Do you have the courage to do that?

Are you brave enough to lead authentically by embracing your courageous fire?

If your answer is yes, it's time to head to chapter one, where we'll discuss how you can spark your fire by exploring the various forms of courage. Courage is not linear; there's more than one type of courage, and once you understand this, everything else will start to make sense as you develop your courageous fire.

It's time to step into courage!

References

Society for Human Resource Management (2023, December 12). Survey: 84 percent of U.S. workers blame bad managers for creating unnecessary stress. Welcome to SHRM. https://www.shrm.org/about/press-room/survey-84-percent-u-s-workers-blame-bad-managers-creating-unnecessary-stress

Althouse, T. *Courageous Leadership Quotes.*

https://www.goodreads.com/quotes/tag/courageous-leadership

Daskal, L. (2016) *What Leadership Is Not.*

https://www.lollydaskal.com/leadership/what-leadership-is-not/

Chapter 1

The Spark Within

———— ❦ ❦ ————

As we journey through life, every one of us carries a spark within, a radiant core that holds the potential for something truly remarkable. It's this flicker of determination that propels us to face our fears, embrace change, and strive for greatness. This spark is the essence of your courage, and it lives within you, dormant, waiting to be ignited.

When it's ignited, the fun begins.

Nelson Mandela once said:

"The brave man is not he who does not feel afraid, but he who conquers that fear."

Finding your courage isn't easy because in order for it to reveal itself, you need to first acknowledge the fear you feel. Nobody likes admitting they're afraid of something, but our courage actually comes from overcoming fear. It's human nature, and the truth is, we all have fears, and we should own them as they show we're truly authentic.

Whatever it is that drives you to overcome your fear is your spark.

In this chapter, you'll explore the "flame" that sparks your courage, uncovering its multifaceted dimensions. It's important to understand how courage reveals itself in various forms, each with its own unique power, and you'll start by developing your understanding of each type. There are six types of courage that will be your companions on your courageous journey: physical, social, moral, emotional, intellectual, and spiritual.

As we dive deeper, you'll come to understand that courage isn't simply about acting with grandeur. It's not solely about scaling mountains or facing down adversaries, although physical courage certainly encompasses this. Instead, it's about summoning the strength to tackle life's everyday challenges, standing up for what you believe in, navigating your emotions, and opening your mind to new horizons.

Throughout this chapter, you'll be introduced to inspirational figures from various walks of life. These are people who have already walked the path of courage with their unwavering determination and resolve. By learning from their stories, you'll gain invaluable insights into what it means to be truly courageous.

It's important to remember that this chapter is not just about admiring the courage of others. It's about feeling inspired and discovering your own inner spark. Courage is patiently waiting for you to fan it into a blazing fire as you explore strategies and techniques to motivate and guide you in finding and nurturing your inner strength.

Throughout, you'll be invited to reflect on your own life, your dreams, and the challenges you face. It's time to embrace your spark within and enable it to light your path in ways you never thought possible. Courage isn't the absence of fear; it's triumph over it. Courage is the win!

It's time to let your inner spark roar and embrace the courage within as you journey toward the extraordinary.

What Are the Six Types of Courage?

Courage is complex. There are different ways to show courage, and there are also different types of courage. When I think of courage, I think about people delivering aid to others following a natural disaster or by entering a war zone. In both cases, the people act without knowing what to expect—anything could happen. Yet their determination to help overcomes the fear of the unknown. Of course, this is a heroic act, but not all courage is the same.

Can you remember a time that you showed courage?

Even if you can't think of something straight away, I guarantee you will have shown courage several times. We show courage, for example, in childhood, when we take our first step, go to school, or make friends. They are all acts of courage, no matter how big or small.

Courage helps us develop in so many ways. It helps us feel a sense of belonging to others and promotes a sense of community. It can also increase decision-making skills and encourage others to be responsible for their own success and failures. It gives us that accountability, which we take with us when we take on a leadership role. To me, there's no doubt—courage also helps us make contributions and master competence cognitively, socially, spiritually, and physically.

As we explore courageous leadership at a deeper level, it's essential to understand and appreciate the six types of courage. Developing your knowledge of them will ensure you have a deeper understanding of courage and what it means. Only then can you start to understand what ignites it.

The six types of courage include:

1. **Physical courage** – This is the ability to confront physical challenges or threats with determination. Physical courage helps you develop your resilience, physical strength, and awareness. It's the brave firefighter rushing into a burning building, the motivated athlete pushing for the gold, or the resilient patient enduring a challenging medical procedure. Physical courage is about conquering the tangible challenges you face in your life.

2. **Social courage** – This is what people conform to and what they believe is "normal" to prevent feeling embarrassed or excluded in society. It's not uncommon to follow a particular path because you feel you should follow it rather than a path you want to follow. Social courage stands as a beacon of authenticity because it is the courage to express your true self, to voice your opinions when they matter most, and to stand up for what you believe in, even if it means standing alone. Social courage is an excellent leadership skill, as it helps you lead the way through difficult and challenging change and uncertainty without wavering.

3. **Moral courage** – This means you are committed to your principles and values, even when you face ethical dilemmas or societal pressure. We all have morals, and moral courage means that you do what you feel is the right thing to do based on your values. It's the whistleblower who exposes wrongdoing, the activist advocating for justice, or the leader who refuses to compromise their integrity.

4. **Emotional courage** – Negative emotions are not easy to navigate, but this type of courage opens you up to experiencing positive emotions despite the risk of experiencing negative ones. It's important to learn to experience both effectively rather than simply ignoring how you feel. Emotional courage is about confronting your inner fears, doubts, and vulnerabilities and accepting that they don't make you weak. It's having the strength to express your feelings, confront emotional wounds, and embrace change, even when the outcome is uncertain.

5. **Intellectual courage** – This type of courage is thought-provoking. We all value knowledge and innovation, and intellectual courage is the force that pushes us to question the status quo, seek new solutions, and expand new horizons. It's the scientist challenging established theories, the entrepreneur trailblazing ideas, and the student unafraid to explore new realms of knowledge, even if it

means making mistakes from time to time. As long as we learn from them, that's the main thing.

6. **Spiritual courage** – Spiritual courage encourages us to explore the profound questions of existence and meaning. It helps to build up resilience and strength as you question these things, including your purpose and your faith. It's the courage to seek inner peace, to deal with life's mysteries, and to connect with something greater than us, whether through religion, philosophy, or self-contemplation.

And those are the six types of courage. Each type holds a unique power, and together, they can guide your leadership journey. While it's important to acknowledge your courage, you don't need to excel in all forms of it simultaneously. You should naturally focus on one or two at a time. You just need to recognize how the different types of courage can collectively fuel your fire and leadership journey.

Courage is not static. It's a personal quality that needs to be developed, shaped, and nurtured, especially when you're in a leadership role. Knowing about these different types of leadership is key, as you need to learn how to harness them to create positive change in your life and the lives of others.

Inspirational People

News flash! I'm not the first person to act courageously, and neither are you. People have shown courage for thousands of years. We have made progress historically with specific acts of courage that have been crucial in shaping the world as we know it today. We've mentioned the different types of courage above, but a courageous person shows a combination of the types of courage. They show confidence and resilience, a strong sense of purpose, are willing to take risks if it means standing up for things they truly believe in, and also have a strong moral compass.

Let's consider four people in history who have shown all these attributes and truly embodied their courageous fire.

Martin Luther King, Jr.

As a civil rights and racial equality activist, Martin Luther King, Jr. is well-known for his "I Have A Dream" speech, as he campaigned tirelessly for equality. He showed courage because, regardless of being threatened with violence or arrested, he never backed down and continued to fight for the things he believed in.

He was committed to the cause and determined to make a difference. He was inspirational to others because his courage prompted others to stand up for the things they believed in. He was assassinated in 1968, but his legacy continues. He is remembered for his bravery and courage.

Rosa Parks

Rosa Parks played a crucial role in the American civil rights movement. Her courage is remembered after she made a stand against racial segregation when she refused to give up her seat on a bus in Alabama. This sparked further protests and ultimately resulted in the end of racial segregation on public transportation. She became an icon in the fight for civil rights. Her courage shows that if just one person is willing to make a stand, they can make a difference.

Jackie Robinson

The courageous Jackie Robinson was the first African American to play Major League Baseball when he signed for the Brooklyn Dodgers on April 15, 1947. Prior to this, African Americans played in their own separate league, so Robinson is renowned for breaking this barrier. He showed tremendous courage throughout his career, and although he received death threats, racist chants, and hate mail, Robinson stayed committed to his team.

He was awarded the Rookie of the Year Award in his first year and became the first African American to receive the National League Most Valuable Player Award in 1949 for the most stolen bases, achieving a career-high 124 RBI and hitting a .342 average. Following his baseball career, Robinson campaigned for equal rights for all Americans and was supported by many who admired and respected him.

Nelson Mandela

Nelson Mandela undoubtedly dedicated his whole life to fighting for equality and justice against racial discrimination. Born in South Africa in 1918 and into an oppressive system, he never gave up the fight despite being arrested multiple times for standing up for the things he believed in. He spent twenty-seven years in prison and was released in 1990. In 1994, he was the first Black president of South Africa. He's one of the most significant figures worldwide, recognized for his courage and determination, which inspired millions of people. He was also awarded the Nobel Peace Prize for his courageous leadership efforts.

Arthur Ashe

Tennis player Arthur Ashe goes down in history for being the first Black man to win the US Open, despite the barriers that stood in his way. Ashe became known for his great backhand and hammering service in the world of tennis and made his way, rising through the ranks. Born in the South and segregated from White people, he went on to break down barriers by dominating the sport before becoming a fierce activist for civil rights. His win at the US Open in 1968 led to the desegregation of tennis. He went on to win the Australian Open in 1970 and Wimbledon in 1975.

There's a lot that can be said for Arthur Ashe, but he was ultimately regarded as an eloquent activist for an array of causes. He used his sports celebrity status as a platform for social action. He led the way and fought for economic empowerment and AIDS awareness and spoke in opposition to Apartheid, in addition to the civil rights movement. He is truly a courageous leader who never stopped fighting for racial and social justice.

While there are many people historically who have made a difference, there are also some modern influences that we can consider. For example, authors such as Stephen King and J.K. Rowling would not have published their books if they were without courage. They are now both a true inspiration to other aspiring authors.

Stephen King was struggling and had very little money when he started writing from his trailer. He received more than sixty rejection letters for a short story, and his best-selling book, *Carrie*, was rejected more than a dozen times. He showed resilience and courage by not giving up and is a major success, as many of his books have since been turned into movies. Continuing to pursue his dreams certainly paid off as it did, too, for *Harry Potter* author J.K. Rowling. In 1994, she was living on government aid, freshly divorced, and struggling to feed her baby. She typed out each version using a typewriter, as she couldn't afford a computer or the cost of photocopying. By 1997, she'd sold her first book, *Harry Potter and the Philosopher's Stone* (also referred to as *The Sorcerer's Stone)*. The book was rejected by twelve different publishers before Bloomsbury decided to give it a chance—but they really didn't expect it to do as well as it did. Her courage was ignited by her love of writing, and now, due to her courage, determination, and resilience, *Harry Potter* is huge.

Why Is It Important to Find Your Spark?

Your inner strength is the spark that ignites your courageous fire. It's the source of your courage, the force that propels you forward when faced with adversity, and the unwavering belief that you can overcome any challenge.

Embracing my courage is something I had to learn. I had to align myself with my values and beliefs and find my inner strength. *But how do you find this inner strength, and how can it become the catalyst for your courageous journey?*

Your inner strength ignites your motivation. When you recognize the ever-flowing source of determination within you, you are more inclined to set ambitious goals and chase your dreams. It's this inner conviction that fuels your desire to overcome obstacles and keep pushing forward, even when the path is uneven.

Moreover, your inner strength enables you to brave the inferno of doubt and uncertainty that often accompanies significant endeavors. When your inner spark is ablaze, you become more resilient in the face of setbacks, more adaptable to change, and more willing to take risks.

Ultimately, your inner strength gives rise to your courageous fire. It's the catalyst that transforms you into an extraordinary leader. When you harness your inner strength, you develop the confidence to lead with conviction, the resilience to withstand adversity, and the authenticity to inspire others.

Remember, your inner strength is the foundation on which your courageous journey is built. It's that spark that pushes you toward greatness, the unwavering belief in your ability to make a difference, and the courage to step boldly into the unknown. It's time to embrace your inner spark. Nurture it, let it grow, and let it guide you on your path to courageous leadership.

Many things inspire us throughout our lives, and this includes the people we encounter along the way. There are many people in my life, events, and experiences that have shaped my perspectives, ignited the fire within me, and helped me find my inner spark. That reminds me, *did I ever tell you about Skipper?*

The Skipper Story

My family lived in San Francisco, and although my mom was an only child, we were never short of family and friends. She had close adult friends and cousins who we would spend time with on the weekends. Skipper was an older cousin of mine who lived in Richmond, California. He lived in quite a rough neighborhood, and I remember being around ten years old when we (my mom, my older brother, my younger brother, and me) went over to his house.

My older brother, Patrick, and I were hanging out with Skipper and my younger cousin, Pee Wee, who was a couple of years younger than me, which made him about eight years old. It was dark, and we were just talking. This guy approached Skipper, and Skipper greeted him—he was casual and friendly—like, *"What's up? What's going on?"* and while I don't remember the whole conversation, I do remember the guy pulling out a gun.

I'd never seen a gun before. It was small, silver, and shiny. I didn't really know what to do, but this experience has always stayed with me because I remember my heart dropped. I was in a state, thinking, *"What's going to happen?"* I didn't know what to expect and don't even remember the chain of events exactly, but the conversation between my cousin and this person continued calmly. Soon, the interaction ended, and the guy went on his way. That was that.

This experience gave me space in my mind and body to consider the interaction. You see, Skipper was able to read the situation well. He didn't panic and reacted accordingly by looking at the cues and assessing the situation. Things could have been very different if we'd reacted differently, and I still use this experience today. It sparked something in me, so when something happens, I subconsciously go back to that time and space and take a moment to think before reacting, and I don't panic. I read the situation.

Skipper was great at reading situations. When I was about eleven or twelve, a famous singer was coming to a South San Francisco skating rink. It was Janet Jackson, and she was huge at the time, as there weren't many famous young Black singers.

Skipper, Patrick, Pee Wee, and I were dropped off by car, but there was a huge crowd of people waiting. We heard that the venue had stopped letting people in, and we were all told to leave. It later came to light that with all the pushing and shoving outside in the crowds, a person was crushed to death. We were in that space, being pushed and squeezed as the crowd tried to get to the entrance. I lived in the next city, San Francisco, so it meant we had to take the bus to get home.

Skipper led us all to the bus stop, but there were so many people there. When the first bus came by, the driver looked at the crowds of people and drove past without stopping. The second bus did the same. Skipper said, "Let's go," and without asking questions, the rest of us followed. We started walking, and it probably took about fifteen to twenty minutes or more, but we arrived at another bus stop (the one before the stop we'd been waiting at). This bus stop was much quieter with no people there, so the bus stopped, and we got on. As we approached the busy bus stop, the bus continued without stopping, but we got home (luckily).

There's no doubt that Skipper had the strategies and tools that allowed him to see beyond a crisis and succeed. He didn't panic, took space to think and assess the situation, and used these things as momentum to help keep us safe and get us all to safety.

Most recently, in the school district where I lead as a superintendent, I attended the graduation event for our alternative education school. The ceremony had gone on without a hitch—it was great, and when it was all over, I headed over to my car through the parking lot. I heard what I thought were firecrackers coming out of the street to my left. I soon realized they were actually gunshots. A car was driving in one direction, and someone was running alongside the car, shooting into it. This was happening probably twenty-five feet directly in front of me. It brought me back to that time with Skipper when my heart dropped, but I didn't panic. I stopped. I looked around and assessed the situation, and I maneuvered myself to safety. Skipper certainly helped me find the spark within to succeed, and this has always stayed with me.

How to Ignite Your Spark

Now, let's dive into the practical strategies that unearth your inner strength. These approaches will help you recognize and harness the spark within, which will ultimately ignite your courageous fire. Mastering what sparks this is the first step to unleashing your firepower:

1. The path to inner strength begins with self-reflection. Take the time to explore your values, passions, and the experiences that have shaped you. Consider important questions, such as:

    a. *What drives you?*

    b. *What are your most cherished beliefs?*

    Self-awareness is the first step in recognizing your inner spark.

2. Challenges and difficulties are not obstacles to your journey but are opportunities to discover your inner strength. When you face adversity, rather than retreating, you should confront it head-on. With each challenge you overcome, your inner spark grows brighter, which is why it's important to embrace your challenges.

3. Clearly define meaningful goals for yourself. These objectives act as beacons, drawing your attention during times of doubt and uncertainty. They give you direction, and when you have a purpose

that resonates deeply with your values, your inner strength becomes a powerful force that drives you forward.

4. Resilience is the ability to bounce back from setbacks. It's closely tied to inner strength and cements the idea that you should never give up. Cultivate resilience by developing a positive mindset, learning from failures, and viewing setbacks as opportunities for growth. Dust yourself off and try again.

5. Building inner strength doesn't mean going it alone, so don't be afraid to lean on your support network. Seek the support of friends, mentors, or anyone else in your network that can assist you. Sharing your aspirations and challenges with others can provide invaluable encouragement and perspective.

6. Mindfulness techniques, such as meditation and deep breathing, can help you connect with your inner self and tap into your inner strength. These practices enable you to remain calm and centered, even when things seem difficult.

By following these strategies and nurturing your inner spark, you will not only find the motivation to continue on your courageous journey but also discover the extraordinary leader within you. Your inner strength is the spark that lights your path, and with it, you can illuminate the way for others, inspiring them to embrace their own courageous fire.

Reflection Time

Take some time to reflect on your courage. Think about the things that are important to you based on your values and beliefs. Also, take some time to consider what drives or motivates you to succeed.

Use the questions below to help you reflect:

1. *What moments in your life have made you feel most fulfilled and alive?*

2. *What activities or interests bring you the most joy and enthusiasm?*

3. *What core values and beliefs guide your decisions and actions?*

4. *How do you want to positively impact the lives of others, and who do you want to help?*

5. *Can you identify any common themes or patterns in your values, interests, and desired impact?*

6. *What values are nonnegotiable for you, and why are they essential?*

7. *What is your "why"? Why do you want to honor your core values and live with purpose?*

8. *What small steps can you take today to align your actions with your values and your "why"?*

These reflection questions can help you go deeper into the process of discovering your inner spark and finding your purpose.

References

10 Remarkable and Courageous People Who Changed the World. (2023, Jan 2)

https://personalfindev.com/blog/10-remarkable-and-courageous-people-who-

changed-the-world

Arsenault, R. (2020, January 31) *How Arthur Ashe Transformed Tennis—and Athlete Activism.* History.com

https://www.history.com/news/arthur-ashe-black-tennis-champion-us-open-activism-courage

Burns, M. (2023, March 1) *The Secret to Outer Success: Develop Your Inner Strength.*

https://www.linkedin.com/pulse/secret-outer-success-develop-your-inner-strength-michelle-burns/

Burns, S. (2023, March 12) *Steve Jobs On Courage.*

https://www.newtraderu.com/2023/03/12/steve-jobs-on-courage/?utm_content=cmp-true#google_vignette

Elkington, H. *Find Your Inner Strength – 7 Essential Ways to Live Happily.*

https://magnifymind.com/find-your-inner-strength/?utm_content=cmp-true#google_vignette

History.Com (2023, March 29) *Jackie Robinson.*

https://www.history.com/topics/black-history/jackie-robinson#jackie-robinson-s-professional-sports-career

James, G. *77 Motivational Quotes That Will Give You Courage.*

https://www.inc.com/geoffrey-james/77-motivational-quotes-that-will-give-you-courage.html#:~:text=Nelson%20Mandela%3A%20%22Courage%20is%20not,gives%20strength%20to%20the%20body.%22

McDonald, S. (2022, January 1) *The Top Ten Most Inspirational Leaders Who Led With Courage.*

https://www.linkedin.com/pulse/top-ten-most-inspirational-leaders-who-led-courage-sonia/

McDonald, S. (2022, September 13).*Bravery VS Courage: 6 Types Of Courage To Know.*

https://www.linkedin.com/pulse/bravery-vs-courage-6-types-know-sonia-mcdonald-dickson-/

Power of Positivity (2021, June 9) *15 Incredible Ways to Find Strength from Within.*

https://www.powerofpositivity.com/strength-within-find-yours/

Robbins, T. *How to Develop Inner Strength.*

https://www.tonyrobbins.com/business/inner-strength/

Scottberg, E. (2020, June 19) *9 Famous People Who Will Inspire You to Never Give Up.*

https://www.themuse.com/advice/9-famous-people-who-will-inspire-you-to-never-give-up

Swerdloff, M. (2020, September 18) *The Six Types of Courage.*

https://www.michaelswerdloff.com/six-types-courage/

Webb, L. (2023, March 9). *Resilience: How to Build Your Inner Strength.*

https://www.liggywebb.com/resilience-how-to-build-your-inner-strength/

Chapter 2

Embracing the Fear and Uncertainty

————···❧❧···————

How often do you embrace fear and uncertainty?

Now, answer honestly here. For some people, that's never, and that's okay. Don't worry if that's your answer, as it's human nature, and it's important to be honest with yourself. In this chapter, we're going to address the role of fear in your life, consider how you can use it positively, and discuss the relationships between courage and vulnerability. I'll also provide some tips on how to confront and overcome fear while inspiring you with some of my own personal experiences and stories so you can see how I've embraced fear and what lessons I've learned from doing so.

When something is uncertain, and we don't know the outcome, it can be exciting, and yet so many people seem to envision the worst-case scenario rather than the positives when faced with uncertainty. *Have you ever thought about why that is?*

By responding this way, we could be setting ourselves up to fail. It's worth considering why we automatically assume it's negative when we could be planning how to make the best of either outcome. You see, we have the power to change outcomes, and this type of planning (for both the best and worst outcomes) is a valuable trait of a courageous leader.

Success comes from learning to face and deal with your fears. If we don't face challenges and fears, we won't be able to claim success because we'd have no way of measuring it. Most of us don't deal with it most effectively, but that's often because we don't know how. It seems to be in our nature to shy away from our fears rather than acknowledging or facing them.

Sure, you can bury your head in the sand for a while, but *how long can you stay like that?* Or more to the point, *why would you want to?* Fear is restrictive, but soon, you'll need space to breathe. I understand just how limiting it can be and why.

I understand that fear is a strange feeling, as it can be extremely debilitating. Fear often causes us to experience a series of emotions, including worry, stress, and anxiety, and these things can impact us in a variety of ways. With that in mind, I want you to consider the question below.

Why do we allow fear to control the actions we take in our lives?

You may not know the answer to that just yet, but it's an interesting question that I want you to keep in mind as you make your way through this chapter. Also, think back to a time when you faced a fear or overcame a barrier that was preventing you from progressing. *How did that make you feel?*

When we embrace fear, we learn something, and the very act of overcoming something helps to build our resilience when it comes to tricky situations. The more we overcome, the more confident we feel. Next time we're faced with such a situation, it doesn't seem so scary, and therefore, we're willing to take action because we have the courage, which is often fueled by the confidence we felt last time. The courage and confidence we feel from overcoming our fear is certainly something that can improve our leadership skills and strengthen us as courageous leaders. We'll talk about this more as the chapter progresses.

To be courageous, you have to undergo a mindset shift to help you view something you fear as being a challenge that you're ready to face and uncertainty as something to be excited about. We'll get to how soon, but let's start by talking about how you can address the role of fear in your life.

Address the Role of Fear in Our Lives

Fear can prevent you from doing the things you want to do because you feel scared, *but why do we feel this?* Fear is unique. We all feel it in different ways about different things, but there is one thing we have in common: Fears can become a barrier for everyone. It often feels easier to give up and avoid your fear rather than face it. But if you prolong dealing with fear, it doesn't serve you because the fear doesn't go away. It simply prevents you from doing what needs to be done. It's, therefore, important to address how fear can negatively impact your life and stop you from doing the things you should be doing.

Imagine this:

You're driving along a quiet road, and the lights change to red. Rather than waiting, you make a right turn. At the next intersection, they go red again, so you avoid this and make another right. The roads slowly start to get busy, but each time you hit a red light, you make a right turn.

The lights are your "barriers," so every time you make a right turn, you're avoiding the barriers. But if you keep avoiding them, *how are you ever going to get to where you need to be?* There's even a chance you'll get back to where you started. You see, if we refuse to acknowledge or face our barriers, they steer us off our route. This means we may never get to where we want to be because those barriers are dictating where we can go and what we can do. Eventually, you're just going in circles and will not make any progress. You'll stagnate.

It's time to stop fear from being a dictator in your life and start using it to fuel your flame of courage. Let's dive deeper into this.

Fear is a silent partner that often casts shadows over our aspirations. This book is about succeeding and developing the courage to overcome anything that stands in your way, so we must learn how to deal with fear—you can't let this take over your life. Fear is the uninvited guest that, at times, stops us from achieving the things we want to achieve. But *what makes fear so formidable?*

When fear steps into the spotlight, it invades our thoughts and emotions. I use the term 'invade' because it appears and tries to take over, even though we don't want it there - fear isn't exactly welcomed. It's the uneasy queasiness we feel before we take on the uncertainties and stand at the crossroads of the unknown. It's the subtle whisper of self-doubt on your abilities.

When the path ahead seems ambiguous, fear eagerly paints vivid worst-case scenarios. It's the discomfort of not knowing what you feel, but the truth is, we can't possibly know everything in life. This is something we all have to accept. It's that lack of self-belief because we just don't think the good things are going to happen. Life is intertwined with uncertainty because none of us really know what lies ahead for us.

Fear becomes a barrier that often flies to new heights. It advises us to be cautious when it's time to be audacious. It sews seeds of self-doubt that offer potential—we just don't see it. It's not just an emotional response; it impedes your progress when life is all about making progress and growth. When fear becomes the architect of your decisions, it constructs walls around the opportunities trying to present themselves to you, stifling growth and restraining the boundless potential within.

Stress is one of the most common consequences of fear, and if your stress levels hit the extreme, you can suffer from numerous health issues, including a weakened immune system, high blood pressure, and diabetes, and it can also impact your heart health. Too much stress weakens your immune system, and it can cause anxiety. Learning to recognize, cope with, and overcome your fears can help prevent stress, which improves your physical and mental health. There's no doubt that if you want to be a courageous and impactful leader, you and your health are a priority—they matter. You matter.

As you navigate life, it's important to consider the cost of letting fear choreograph your choices. *Who's really in control here?* When unexamined, fear simply stands in your way as it undermines the richness that life, with all its uncertainties, has to offer. Fear can strain relationships, cause you to avoid achieving the things you want to achieve, stop you from thinking clearly, and prevent you from living a healthy lifestyle.

The first step toward dismantling the grip of fear is to first acknowledge it—don't ignore it. Then, by understanding the emotions it evokes and the barriers it constructs, you gain the power to dismantle its grip, one finger at a time. Knowledge and understanding go a long way. It empowers you by helping you tap into your courageousness.

Learning to overcome your fears is a journey of self-discovery that recognizes how fear doesn't need to influence your decisions and actions. It's important to explore strategies to untangle fear's web, transforming it from a hindrance into a catalyst for courage and growth.

So, address the role fear plays in your life and its impact, and remember, the path to your fullest potential lies beyond fear, and that path is waiting for you to take courageous steps forward.

But how do courage and vulnerability fit into this?

Discuss the Relationship between Courage and Vulnerability

Courage and vulnerability are connected. They're the narrative of strength and openness, and by understanding these nuances, you can unravel the relationship between them.

Courage is at the heart of audacity, the inner flame that propels us to confront challenges head-on. It's the unwavering trembles and tallness in the face of adversity, speaking our truth even when our voice trembles, and taking on unknown journeys. Courage is a testament to resilience and a declaration of our commitment to growth.

On the other side of the spectrum lies vulnerability. At one time, vulnerability was seen to be a sign of weakness, but in truth, it's the authentic unveiling of oneself—the willingness to expose our true feelings, aspirations, and fears. It's the raw honesty and authenticity that connects us on a human level, makes us relatable, and fosters empathy as we make genuine connections.

But how do courage and vulnerability work hand in hand? How would you characterize their relationship?

Vulnerability is often an asset, as owning it shows courage. There's nothing better than being able to relate to those you admire, for instance, realizing that you and that person you admire have experienced similar hardships or difficulties. It's the acknowledgment that embracing the unknown, taking risks, and forging genuine connections require a willingness to be vulnerable. It's the ability to bear the truth proudly and openly, showing our human side. True courage lies not in the absence of vulnerability but in having the audacity to show it.

Consider the act of sharing your authentic self with the world. This vulnerability is often misconceived as frailty, but in fact, it's a profound act of courage. It's a strength. It's the courage to be seen, flaws and all, because we're not perfect, and that's fine. It helps us to continue to forge powerful connections as vulnerability, in this sense, becomes a gateway to profound courage.

When faced with uncertainty, courage propels us to step forward, even when the path is shrouded in ambiguity. This requires a vulnerability that acknowledges our uncertainties and imperfections. It's the recognition that growth and discovery often unfold in the uncharted territories of vulnerability, and if I'm honest, this recognition helped me grow into a courageous leader. I believe it can do the same for you.

Courage is not a facade but more of a dynamic force that thrives in openness. Our vulnerabilities allow courage to take root, enabling us to express our true selves, admit our fears, and strive for authenticity. Courage and vulnerability are closely linked, creating strength and candidness. It's an acknowledgment that true courage isn't a shield against vulnerability but an act that embraces it.

It's common for people to avoid discussing their vulnerabilities because they fear showing this side of themselves. This allows your vulnerabilities to become barriers that keep you from progressing. Revealing ourselves can be tricky business because we don't want to be judged, rejected, or feel inadequate because of these things.

Your courage demands you to use those vulnerabilities as a positive force. It wants you to be courageous and disclose vulnerabilities, as this is a powerful balance between openness and resilience to face what we fear the most. As we continue our journey, let's recognize that the most courageous moments often arise from the vulnerable spaces within us, fostering authenticity and genuine connection. Ultimately, vulnerability is the fuel to your courageous fire, and the clear message here is that you should not ignore it but embrace it.

Reflect and Unmask Your Fears

Take some time to consider the questions below and reflect on your own fears, vulnerabilities, and barriers.

1. What goals or aspirations in your life are currently accompanied by a sense of fear or uncertainty?

2. Can you identify specific barriers that seem to hinder your progress in these areas? Take a moment to list them.

3. Reflect on the origins of these fears and barriers. Are they rooted in past experiences, external expectations, or self-doubt?

4. What patterns or common themes do you notice among the fears and barriers you've identified? Are there recurring motifs across different aspects of your life?

5. Consider the relationship between vulnerability and fear. How does the act of revealing your true self contribute to feelings of fear or uncertainty?

6. In what ways can you reframe these barriers as opportunities for growth and learning?

7. Are there specific steps you can take to confront and overcome these fears? List one or two actionable steps for each reframed barrier.

8. How might expressing gratitude for the insights gained during this reflection impact your mindset and approach to these challenges?

9. Think about times in the past when you've overcome fear or vulnerability. What strengths did you tap into, and how can you apply those lessons to your current situation?

10. Consider the concept of courageous fire. What would it mean for you to fan the flames of your courageous fire, and how could this propel you toward your goals?

Reflecting on your own fears, vulnerabilities, and barriers encourages you to confront and reframe the challenges you face and use them as opportunities for resilience and growth.

Embracing the Fear: My Story

Thirteen years ago, my world was shaken by a devastating loss—the passing of my younger brother, Elliott. He was only thirty-three and had so much more life to live. His battle with a rare blood disorder meant his body started attacking his vital organs, and despite our hopes and prayers, he succumbed to organ failure in 2011. As I grappled with the weight of grief, I found myself having to head back home to San Francisco from Southern California alongside my pregnant wife to help my mother put together the services for my brother.

I was confronted with fears and concerns about returning to my childhood home in San Francisco that I hadn't even realized I had. It's funny; the term "home" is a place that gives us comfort and makes us feel at ease, but my hometown is very different from the home I came to create with my wife and family. I was raised in an inner-city neighborhood of San Francisco, Hunters Point, by what used to be Candlestick Park, where the San Francisco 49ers and Giants played. It was predominantly populated by Black families, and I was intimately familiar with the tight-knit community that had shaped my upbringing. Yet, as I stood among the mourners at my brother's funeral, I couldn't ignore the sensation of apprehension I felt in my gut.

You see, my wife is White—a fact that set her apart in the sea of familiar faces at the funeral. In fact, I don't remember any other White person being there. At the time, in a community where interracial relationships were still met with skepticism and scrutiny, I couldn't shake off the feelings I felt—I knew that covert judgment and ridicule were lingering. I was questioning whether our presence would be accepted or if we would face the whispered criticisms and sideways glances of those with strong views about such things. After all, I had been away from "home" for more than twenty years.

Despite my trepidation, I knew that I had to confront my fears head-on. I mean, we had no choice, and my wife seemed fine with everything. As we navigated the solemn rituals of the funeral and subsequent celebration of life, I abruptly arrived at a realization—I was no longer the impressionable boy who had grown up in the shadows of societal expectations.

With each step I took beside my wife, I felt a surge of courage and determination. *This is who I am*, I reminded myself, unapologetic in my authenticity. As we embraced friends and family, it was obvious to me that the bonds of community ran deeper than any superficial judgments or prejudices.

At that moment, in embracing my truth and standing tall in the face of fear, I reclaimed a sense of belonging and connection to others that transcended the boundaries of race or background. The acceptance and understanding enveloped us, reaffirming the power of vulnerability and courage in fostering genuine human connection. That realization was an influential moment for me—it was powerful. The truth is that things change, but we must be courageous to impact that change.

Now, more than a decade later, I look back on that instrumental moment in my life with gratitude and clarity. By embracing my fears and embracing my true self, I not only forged deeper connections with those around me but also rediscovered the resilience and strength that reside within each of us. In the end, it was the courage to be vulnerable that brought me closer to the community where I was raised and reaffirmed the power of authenticity in fostering meaningful relationships.

Remember, embracing your true self, despite the fear of judgment or rejection, is a powerful act of liberation and self-affirmation. Dare to be unapologetically you, knowing that true connections and belonging await those who dare to stand tall in their authenticity.

How to Confront and Overcome Fears

In leadership, cultivating your courageous fire is intrinsically tied to confronting and overcoming fears. True leadership doesn't thrive in the absence of fear but emerges triumphantly in the flames of your courage. As you tend your courageous fire, consider each fear you confront as being the fuel to your flames. You can use this fuel to light your way.

Overcoming fears is the process of stoking the flames as you trailblaze leadership. When you face your fears head-on, you tap into your growing strength and resilience that defines authentic leadership. The vulnerability of acknowledging your fears is the very spark that ignites your courage, and the more you overcome them, the more your fire roars and gains momentum. Every fear you conquer becomes a stepping stone that pushes you toward greater heights of leadership prowess.

Let's consider the relationship between overcoming fears and building your courageous fire. . . .

Each fear confronted demonstrates your courage and is a declaration that you are willing to head into the unknown. This willingness to confront fears not only deepens your self-awareness but also fortifies the very core of your leadership skills and abilities. It's in these moments of facing fears that your courageous fire burns at its brightest, illuminating your path and inspiring those around you.

The journey to overcoming your fears is both empowering and transformative. If you want to be a courageous leader, you must equip yourself with strategies that light up your path to courage. There are some simple strategies you can adopt to help you conquer the fears that challenge you and cast light on the connection between vulnerability, resilience, and the radiant flames of your courageous fire. Use these as your guiding lights that lead you toward the triumph of courageous leadership.

- The first step is to identify and name your fears. Write them down, acknowledging their presence. This simple act can diminish their power.

- Challenge negative thoughts associated with your fears. Reframe them into positive affirmations that reinforce your capability and resilience.

- Divide your fears into smaller, manageable steps. Tackling them incrementally makes the process less daunting and builds a sense of accomplishment.

- Share your fears with trusted colleagues, mentors, or friends. Sometimes, verbalizing your fears diminishes their weight, and external perspectives can provide valuable insights.

- Visualize yourself successfully overcoming your fears. Visualization can be a powerful tool to boost confidence and create a positive mindset.

- Understand that setbacks are a natural part of facing fears. Instead of viewing them as failures, see them as opportunities for learning and growth.

- Acknowledge and celebrate each step forward, no matter how small. Recognizing progress boosts your confidence and reinforces the notion that you can overcome challenges.

- Resilience is a key component of overcoming fears. Cultivate your resilience by focusing on your strengths, learning from experiences, and adapting to change.

As you integrate these strategies into your leadership journey, remember that you should not allow the courageous fire within you to be extinguished by fear. There's no doubt that it's forged and strengthened through the intentional act of facing and overcoming it. While you may feel deflated at times, it's important to get back up and spark those flames again. As I've mentioned before, good leadership is not reflected in the absence of our fears but in our ability to confront them with courage.

Overcoming my fears has taught me that the dark shadows of uncertainty provide me with both an experience and an opportunity for personal growth. As I observed and reflected on the impact of this process, I learned that vulnerability is certainly not a weakness but a source of authentic strength that provides fuel to the flames. In life and leadership, we have to step out of our comfort zone, and by acknowledging my own fears, I was able to push through the discomfort and bounce back. I know I'm capable of dealing with almost any situation I face, so there's no need for me to fear the "what-ifs." My experiences have illuminated the connection between vulnerability and the vibrant flames of my courageous fire and provided me with confidence. I understand that true leadership is forged in the very act of facing and conquering any situation, circumstance, or thing that stands in my way.

If you cultivate your courageous fire, it will grow, just like mine has.

References

5 Strategies for Confronting Fear. (2016, March 10) Exploringyourmind.com

https://exploringyourmind.com/5-strategies-confronting-fear/

5 Things You Never Knew About Fear. (2020, October).

https://www.nm.org/healthbeat/healthy-tips/emotional-health/5-things-you-never-knew-about-fear

5 Ways Which Fears Can Negatively Impact Your Life. (2016) Better Health Solutions.

https://www.betterhealthsolutions.org/5-ways-fears-can-negatively-impact-life/

10 Ways to Fight Your Fears. (2024, June 13).

https://www.nhsinform.scot/healthy-living/mental-wellbeing/fears-and-phobias/10-ways-to-fight-your-fears/

Debevoise, ND. (2024, April 22) Courage And Vulnerability: 3 Ways To Face Fears As A Purposeful Leader. Forbes.

https://www.forbes.com/sites/nelldebevoise/2024/04/22/courage-and-vulnerability-3-ways-to-face-fears-as-a-purposeful-leader/

Hohlbaum, C L. (2015, July 6) *Why Vulnerability Takes Courage.* Psychology Today.

https://www.psychologytoday.com/us/blog/the-power-slow/201507/why-vulnerability-takes-courage

How To Be Brave: Understanding And Overcoming Fear. (2024, April 18). Better Help.

https://www.betterhelp.com/advice/how-to/how-to-be-brave-and-overcome-fear/

How to Manage Anxiety and Fear. Mental Health Foundation.

https://www.mentalhealth.org.uk/explore-mental-health/publications/how-overcome-anxiety-and-fear

LaBier, D. (2013, March 4) *Why Your Fears Shape So Much of Your Life.* Psychology Today.

https://www.psychologytoday.com/us/blog/the-new-resilience/201303/why-your-fears-shape-so-much-your-life

Perry, E. (2022, December 28) *The purpose of fear and how to overcome it*

https://www.betterup.com/blog/purpose-of-fear

Roche, MK. (2023, March 8). *How Being Vulnerable is Inspiring, Courageous, and Necessary.*

https://www.linkedin.com/pulse/how-being-vulnerable-inspiring-courageous-necessary-kingston-roche/

Saviuc, L. *9 Ways to Overcome Fear and Live With Courage.* Purpose Fairy

https://www.purposefairy.com/87470/overcome-fear/

Todorovic, JS. (2022, September 22). *Fear of Leadership is Real - Here's How You Can Overcome It.*

https://www.linkedin.com/pulse/fear-leadership-real-heres-how-you-can-overcome-john-s-todorovic/

Chapter 3

Navigating Adversity

———— ❀❀ ————

"Success is to be measured not so much by the position that one has reached in life as by the obstacles which he has overcome while trying to succeed." ~ Booker T. Washington

It's a fact. If we want to succeed in life, we have to overcome obstacles. Adversity isn't uncommon—many of us face many challenges and obstacles in life that are, in fact, adversities, but it's our courage that we often use to overcome them. In the vast landscape of life, adversity is an arduous force that challenges our resolve and tests the depth of our resilience.

Adversity is something that most of us have to face from time to time, and it comes in many forms. In this chapter, we'll explore the depths of adversity, exploring its multifaceted nature and shedding light on the transformative power it holds. As we work through it, we'll uncover its manifestations and learn to recognize its subtle presence in our lives. We'll also draw inspiration from people who have triumphed over adversity and discover the resilience that lies within each of us.

Through personal stories, reflections, and practical strategies, let's begin to navigate adversity, emerging stronger, more resilient, and empowered to face whatever life may bring.

If you can overcome adversity, you can accomplish anything!

What Is Adversity?

We've all faced adversities in life. As I've mentioned already, adversity can be a force that casts its shadow over our lives, challenging both our resolve and resilience. It encompasses the trials, tribulations, and setbacks we encounter on our journey, often arriving unexpectedly and shaking the very foundations of our existence. Adversity can take many forms, from personal struggles and setbacks to external challenges and obstacles. It may manifest as a loss, a failure, a setback, or a sudden change in circumstances.

Regardless of its form, it's important to recognize that adversity presents us with a profound opportunity for growth, resilience, and transformation. It's the crucible that shapes our character, making us stronger, wiser, and more resilient people. It takes practice to start recognizing the opportunities we're presented with, but in essence, while adversity can be a negative, it's also an opportunity for personal growth and self-discovery.

Now, adversity is not always easy to recognize, *so let's talk about how we can recognize adversity.* Let's consider this and make recognizing it really easy.

How Can I Recognize Adversity?

Recognizing adversity requires a keen awareness of the challenges and obstacles we encounter on our journey through life. While adversity can manifest in various forms, there are common signs and patterns that can help us identify its presence.

One key indicator of adversity is a sense of struggle or difficulty in achieving our goals or fulfilling our responsibilities. This may include facing unexpected obstacles, experiencing setbacks or failures, or encountering resistance from external forces.

Adversity often brings feelings of frustration, disappointment, or despair, as well as a sense of powerlessness or hopelessness. It can also manifest in physical symptoms such as stress, anxiety, or fatigue. By paying attention to these signs and acknowledging the presence of adversity in our lives, we can begin to confront and overcome its challenges. This section will explore the various forms that adversity can take, from personal struggles and setbacks to external challenges and obstacles. By gaining a deeper understanding of adversity and its impact on our lives, we can develop the resilience and strength needed to navigate its turbulent waters.

Don't Let Adversity Stop You. They Didn't!

I wanted to spend some time giving examples of those who have broken down adversity barriers to really cement the true meaning of adversity. The truth is, if we want to affect change and make progress, navigating adversity is something we have to do constantly and consistently.

It's a fact—if you let adversity stop you, then progress will never happen. If the people we're about to discuss didn't navigate adversity effectively, we probably wouldn't be talking about them today.

Joseph Rainey: Breaking Barriers in Congress

In the era of Reconstruction following the Civil War, Joseph Rainey emerged as a beacon of hope and resilience. Born into slavery in South Carolina in 1832, Rainey defied the odds stacked against him and rose to become the first Black person to win a seat in the United States House of Representatives.

Rainey's journey to Congress was marked by adversity at every turn, but he never gave up. Despite facing discrimination and systemic racism, he pursued education and self-improvement, working as a barber and successful businessman. In 1862, when the Reconstruction era opened the door for Black political participation, Rainey seized the opportunity and ran for a seat in the House of Representatives.

His path to Congress was fraught with challenges, including voter suppression tactics and violent intimidation. Yet, Rainey remained undeterred, rallying support from fellow Black citizens and allies in the fight for equality. In December 1870, Rainey made history when he was sworn in as the first Black member of the U.S. House of Representatives.

Throughout his tenure in Congress, Rainey continued to advocate for the things he believed in, such as the rights and liberties of African Americans. He championed civil rights legislation and economic empowerment initiatives. His resilience in the face of adversity paved the way for future generations of Black leaders and inspired countless others to pursue their dreams, regardless of the obstacles in their path.

Joseph Rainey's legacy serves as a testament to the power of resilience, determination, and unwavering courage in the pursuit of justice and equality. Despite the adversities he faced, Rainey refused to let them stop him from making history and leaving a mark on American democracy. His story serves as a beacon of hope and inspiration for all who dare to dream and defy the odds.

Fritz Pollard: Trailblazing on the Gridiron

In American sports history, Fritz Pollard stands as a trailblazer whose spirit and unwavering determination shattered barriers and paved the way for future generations of athletes and coaches. Born in Chicago in 1894, Pollard rose to prominence as one of the most electrifying football players of his era and went on to become the first Black coach in the National Football League (NFL).

Pollard's journey to the gridiron was marked by adversity from the outset. Growing up in a segregated society, he faced racial discrimination and prejudice at every turn. Yet, Pollard refused to be defined by the limitations imposed upon him by society, channeling his talents and passion for football into a pursuit of excellence.

As a standout athlete at Brown University, Pollard showcased his exceptional speed, agility, and athleticism, earning recognition as one of the top collegiate football players of his time. Despite his undeniable talent, however, Pollard encountered resistance when he sought opportunities to play professionally in the predominantly White NFL.

Undeterred by the racial barriers that stood in his path, Pollard blazed a trail of his own, becoming one of the first Black players to break into the NFL in 1919. Overcoming prejudice and discrimination, he distinguished himself as a dynamic running back and versatile playmaker, captivating fans with his electrifying performances on the field.

Pollard's impact extended far beyond his achievements as a player. In 1921, he made history once again when he became the first Black coach in the NFL, leading the Akron Pros to a championship victory in his inaugural season. As a coach, Pollard shattered stereotypes and challenged perceptions, proving that excellence knows no color or race; excellence and courage have no bounds.

Throughout his illustrious career, Pollard remained steadfast in his commitment to excellence, resilience, and the pursuit of opportunity. His pioneering achievements paved the way for future generations of Black athletes and coaches, leaving an indelible mark on the landscape of American sports.

Fritz Pollard's legacy serves as a timeless reminder of the power of perseverance, courage, and determination in the face of adversity. Despite the challenges he encountered, Pollard refused to let adversity stop him from realizing his dreams and paving the way for others. His story is a testament to the enduring spirit of resilience and the boundless possibilities that arise when we refuse to be defined by the obstacles in our way.

Gordon Parks: Capturing Dreams on Film

In the world of cinematics, Gordon Parks stands as a towering figure whose groundbreaking work as a filmmaker and photographer transcended racial barriers and reshaped the landscape of American art and culture. But getting there wasn't an easy road.

Born in Fort Scott, Kansas, in 1912, Parks overcame poverty, discrimination, and adversity to become the first Black director of a Hollywood studio film. His journey to the silver screen was marked by perseverance and determination in the face of overwhelming odds. Growing up in a segregated society, he encountered racial prejudice and discrimination from an early age. Despite the challenges he faced, Parks discovered his passion for photography and storytelling, using his camera as a tool for social change and cultural expression.

As a photographer for the Farm Security Administration during the Great Depression, Parks captured the harsh realities of life in America's heartland, shedding light on the struggles of marginalized communities. His iconic images of poverty, segregation, and injustice resonated with audiences across the nation, earning him recognition as one of the preeminent documentarians of his time.

Parks' transition to filmmaking was a natural extension of his storytelling abilities and social consciousness. In 1969, he made history when he directed *The Learning Tree*, becoming the first Black director of a Hollywood studio film. Based on his own semi-autobiographical novel, the film explored themes of race, identity, and adolescence in rural America, earning critical acclaim and cementing Parks' place in cinematic history.

Throughout his prolific career, Parks continued to challenge stereotypes and defy expectations, using his art as a vehicle for social commentary and cultural critique. From his groundbreaking work as a filmmaker to his pioneering contributions to fashion photography and music composition, Parks' legacy transcends the boundaries of any single medium, inspiring generations of artists and activists to confront adversity with creativity, resilience, and unwavering determination.

Gordon Parks' journey from poverty to prominence serves as a testament to the transformative power of art, resilience, and the human spirit. Despite the adversity he faced, Parks refused to be defined by the limitations imposed upon him by society, paving the way for future generations of Black filmmakers and artists. His story is a reminder that our dreams are without boundaries, and with perseverance and passion, anything is possible. So keep on dreaming!

Ruth Simmons: Leading with Courage and Vision

In the world of academia, Ruth Simmons stands out as a visionary leader with an unwavering resolve to shatter barriers and transform the landscape of higher education. Born into humble beginnings in Grapeland, Texas, Simmons defied the odds to become the first Black president of an Ivy League university. This was a major accomplishment and a monumental moment that we should recognize in history.

Simmons' journey to academia was marked by resilience, determination, and an unyielding commitment to excellence. Growing up in the segregated South, she experienced firsthand the injustices of racism and discrimination. Despite facing systemic barriers to education, Simmons pursued higher learning with a fierce determination, earning degrees from Dillard University and Harvard University and completing her PhD at Harvard in Romance languages and literature.

Throughout her career, Simmons distinguished herself as a scholar, educator, and visionary leader. As president of Smith College, she implemented groundbreaking initiatives with confidence to promote diversity, equity, and inclusion, earning national acclaim for her efforts to advance women's education and leadership.

In 2001, Simmons made history when she was appointed president of Brown University, becoming the first Black president of an Ivy League institution. During her tenure, she launched bold initiatives to expand access to higher education, enhance academic excellence, and foster a more inclusive campus community. Under her leadership, Brown University experienced unprecedented growth and transformation, solidifying its reputation as a global leader in education and research.

Simmons' impact extended far beyond this as she emerged as a powerful advocate for social justice, economic opportunity, and the transformative power of education. There's no doubt that her leadership inspired countless people to pursue their dreams and defy the limitations imposed upon them by society.

Her journey from rural Texas to the helm of one of the nation's most prestigious universities is owed to her relentless perseverance, resilience, and visionary leadership. Despite the adversities she faced, Simmons refused to be defined by the limitations of her circumstances, charting a path of excellence and opportunity for future generations. Her story reminds us that with courage, determination, and resolve, we can overcome any obstacle and achieve greatness.

Now that we've explored these extraordinary people, just imagine a world that didn't challenge adversity. The people discussed above fought for what they believed in despite the adversities they faced, and this made them changemakers for future generations. There's no doubt they made an impact on the world and on society. You see, even when we are faced with adversity, there's still hope. You can overcome it. You can break down the barriers that are preventing your progress.

The truth is, we can't and shouldn't allow adversity to prevent us from succeeding and achieving the things we want to achieve! Just like Joseph, Fritz, Gordon, and Ruth, you can and should be using your courage to navigate the adversities you face and influence change.

Take a few moments to think about that.

Reflection Time

Take a moment to reflect on your own encounters with adversity, both those where you emerged victorious and those where you faced challenges:

1. *Recall a Time of Adversity*

   Think back to a specific instance in your life when you were faced with adversity. It could be a personal struggle, a setback at work or school, a health challenge, or a difficult relationship. What were the circumstances surrounding this adversity?

2. *Identify Your Response*

   Reflect on how you responded to this adversity. Did you face it head-on with courage and resilience, or did you feel overwhelmed and unsure of how to proceed? What emotions did you experience during this time?

3. *Lessons Learned from Success*

   If you succeeded in overcoming the adversity, consider what factors contributed to your success. What strengths, skills, or resources did you draw upon? What did you learn about yourself in the process?

4. *Insights from Setbacks*

   If you faced challenges or setbacks in dealing with adversity, reflect on what you learned from these experiences. What obstacles did you encounter, and how did they shape your response? What could you have done differently?

5. *Growth and Resilience*

   Consider how these experiences of adversity have influenced your personal growth and resilience. Have they strengthened your resolve, deepened your self-awareness, or fostered a greater sense of empathy toward others facing similar challenges?

6. _Moving Forward_

Finally, think about how you can apply the lessons learned from these experiences to future encounters with adversity. What strategies can you employ to cultivate resilience, maintain a positive mindset, and navigate challenges with grace and determination?

Don't rush this! Take as much time as you need to reflect on these questions, and remember that facing adversity is an opportunity for growth and self-discovery. Your experiences, both triumphs and challenges, shape who you are and equip you with the strength and resilience needed to overcome life's obstacles.

Building Your Resilience

Resilience is the cornerstone of navigating life's challenges with grace and grit. It's the inner strength that allows us to bounce back from setbacks, adapt to adversity, and thrive in the face of uncertainty. While some people may naturally possess a higher level of resilience, it's certainly a skill that can be cultivated and strengthened over time. That means resilience is something you can develop and improve.

Let's explore practical strategies for building resilience and equipping yourself with the tools to navigate life's ups and downs with resilience and determination:

- Embrace the belief that challenges are opportunities for growth and learning. Adopting a growth mindset allows you to view setbacks as temporary and as opportunities to develop new skills and insights.

- Treat yourself with kindness and compassion, especially during difficult times. Acknowledge your emotions without judgment and remind yourself that it's okay to struggle. Self-compassion fosters resilience by helping you bounce back from setbacks with greater ease.

- Surround yourself with supportive friends, family members, and mentors who can offer encouragement, guidance, and perspective during challenging times. Cultivating strong support networks provides a sense of belonging and strengthens resilience.

- Identify healthy coping mechanisms that help you manage stress and adversity effectively. This may include mindfulness meditation, deep breathing exercises, journaling, or engaging in hobbies and activities that bring you joy.

- Break down large goals into smaller, manageable tasks that are achievable and realistic. Celebrate small victories along the way, and don't be discouraged by setbacks. Setting realistic goals helps build confidence and resilience over time.

- Keep things in perspective by focusing on the bigger picture and reframing challenges as temporary obstacles rather than insurmountable barriers. Cultivate gratitude for the blessings in your life, even during difficult times.

- Practice flexibility and adaptability in your approach to life's challenges. Recognize that change is inevitable and being able to adapt to new circumstances is a key component of resilience.

- Find meaning and purpose in your experiences, even during times of adversity. Connect with your values and beliefs, and use them as guiding principles to navigate life's challenges with integrity and purpose.

- Reflect on past experiences of adversity and identify the lessons learned from these challenges. Use these insights to develop resilience and strengthen your ability to cope with future adversities.

- Prioritize self-care practices that take care of your body, mind, and spirit. This may include getting enough sleep, eating a balanced diet, exercising regularly, and engaging in activities that bring you joy and relaxation.

If you incorporate at least some of these strategies into your daily life (all of them, if you can), you can build resilience and strengthen your inner foundation, empowering yourself to navigate life's challenges with courage, resilience, and grace.

Just remember that resilience is not about avoiding adversity but about facing it head-on and emerging stronger on the other side. It's a test of your inner strength.

My Battle with Adversity

Adversity is a battle, but it's a battle we can win if we make the right choices. I want to share with you one of my experiences with adversity. Growing up in the inner city of San Francisco as a young Black kid was challenging at times, especially when it was time to graduate from high school. In my community, the path after high school seemed simple: Either you went to college (that was a small percentage), or you risked falling into a life of crime or worse (in most cases, this meant prison or ending up dead). For me, college was the only viable option, but that doesn't mean it was an easy road.

When I was admitted to California State University, Long Beach, it came with a condition: I had to attend a Summer Bridge Program. Of course, I did it, I worked hard, and I got in. During the first semester of college, I found myself drowning in five or six classes (that's like all of them), barely scraping by, mostly Fs in my classes. I was more focused on fraternity parties and drinking games than my studies, and looking back, I can see how this was reflected in my grades, but I was young and didn't know how the world worked. Living in the dorms also didn't help my focus.

After that disastrous first semester, I hit rock bottom. While I did better in the second semester, I still had an extremely low GPA and multiple low grades. It wasn't good enough, and at the end of my second year, I was disqualified from the university. It felt like the end of the road for my college dreams—being kicked out was a wake-up call. I could've given up, but deep down, something inside me refused to do so.

I enrolled in the local community college, Long Beach City College, and I was determined to turn things around. I threw myself into my studies with a newfound dedication and discipline. After a year of hard work, I managed to get my grades back on track and was readmitted back into California State University, Long Beach.

This time around, I approached my studies with a newfound sense of purpose. I learned from my mistakes—I wasn't going to waste this second chance. I was more focused, more disciplined, and more determined than ever before. It wasn't easy, but three years later, I proudly walked across the stage to receive my undergraduate degree. It had taken me five years in total, but I had overcome the odds and achieved my goal.

Looking back, I realize adversity is a natural and normal part of life. It's not about avoiding obstacles but about finding the strength and resilience to overcome them. My college journey taught me that success isn't measured by the absence of challenges but by how we respond to them.

I may have stumbled along the way, and maybe I even took the long route, but I never lost sight of my goal. I learned the importance of perseverance, resilience, and grit. And most importantly, I learned that setbacks are not the end of the road but merely detours on the path to success.

Today, when I look back, I'm grateful for the obstacles I faced. They have made me who I am today and taught me valuable lessons that I carry with me in every aspect of my life.

My message to you is:

Adversity may knock us down, but it's how we choose to get back up that defines us. That's what true success is all about!

Bouncing Back from Setbacks

Yes, life is filled with unexpected twists and turns, and setbacks are an inevitable part of the journey. Something I've learned (probably the hard way) is that it's not the setbacks themselves that define us but how we respond to them. It's that ability to bounce back from those setbacks that counts, and while that's not always easy, let's be honest here: It's something we always *must* do to get through life.

It's time to discuss some strategies for resilience and bouncing back from setbacks so you feel equipped with the tools you need to navigate adversity with courage and determination.

The first thing you need to do is acknowledge your emotions. When faced with a setback, it's natural to experience a range of emotions, including frustration, disappointment, and even anger. Instead of suppressing these emotions, allow yourself to acknowledge and process them. Recognizing and validating your feelings is the first step toward resilience; sometimes, we just have to *feel* those emotions before we can move on.

Practicing self-compassion is also a key strategy because we live in a world in which we are ultimately tough on ourselves. Treat yourself with kindness and compassion during times of setbacks. Avoid self-criticism and negative self-talk, as they don't serve you. Instead, offer yourself words of encouragement and support—be your own cheerleader. Remember that setbacks are a normal part of life, and it's okay to struggle.

Many people don't ask for help and support when they need it, but this is a mistake. Don't hesitate to reach out to friends, family members, or mentors for support during difficult times. Sharing your feelings and experiences with others can offer a sense of validation and perspective, as well as provide practical advice and guidance.

Now, this is important, so listen up. Instead of viewing setbacks as failures, reframe them as opportunities for growth and learning. Ask yourself what you can learn from the experience and how it can help you become stronger and more resilient in the future. You also need to set your focus on the things that you can control and work on building your inner strength. While setbacks may be beyond your control, you have power over the aspects of the situation that you can control. Identify actionable steps that you can take to address the setback and move forward in a positive direction.

It's important to practice resilience by engaging in activities that promote well-being, such as mindfulness meditation, exercise, journaling, or spending time in nature. While these activities may not be for everyone, find something that is. Things like this can help you manage stress, gain perspective, and cultivate a sense of inner strength. They also provide valuable thinking time so you can subconsciously process information you've recently learned or help you look at problems from a fresh perspective.

It's common for us to have such high expectations for ourselves, which means we set goals that just aren't realistic. Stop setting yourself up for a fall! To avoid this, be sure to break down your goals into smaller, manageable tasks that are achievable and realistic. Celebrate your small victories along the way, and don't be discouraged by setbacks. Setting realistic goals helps build confidence and resilience over time. The main thing to do when you're bouncing back is to learn from your experiences. Reflect on the lessons learned from setbacks and use them as opportunities for growth and self-improvement. Consider what you can do differently in the future to prevent similar setbacks from occurring.

If you implement these strategies, you will strengthen your resilience and be equipped to bounce back from setbacks with greater ease and confidence. Remember what I told you earlier—setbacks are not the end of the road but merely detours on the path to success. With resilience and determination, you can find your way back to your original path by overcoming any obstacle and emerge stronger on the other side.

As we reach the end of this chapter, it's safe to say we've explored the depths of adversity, uncovering its multifaceted nature and discovering its transformative power. From the personal stories of resilience we reviewed to the practical strategies for navigating life's challenges, we've journeyed through the depths of adversity with courage, resilience, and determination. Now, it's down to you to take these strategies and implement them.

But our exploration doesn't end here. As we move on to the next chapter, let's carry forward the lessons learned and the insights gained from our encounters with adversity. Just as adversity has the power to test our resolve and challenge our resilience, it also has the potential to cultivate kindness, compassion, and courage within us.

This is what we'll focus on in chapter four as we explore the profound impact of kindness and compassion in the face of adversity and go into what it means to be courageously kind. Sometimes, it's the simple acts of compassion that create a ripple effect of positivity and change in the world around us.

Just remember, adversity may test our strength, but it's kindness that truly defines our humanity.

References

14 People Who Broke Barriers to Make Black History Month. NBC News.

https://www.nbcnews.com/news/nbcblk/14-individuals-who-made-black-history-n722051

Adversity. Merriam-Webster.com.

https://www.merriam-webster.com/dictionary/adversity

Building Resilience: How to Bounce Back from Setbacks. Maxme.

https://www.maxme.com.au/insights/building-resilience-how-to-bounce-back-from-setbacks

Building Resilience: Strategies for Bouncing Back from Setbacks and Challenges in Your Career.

https://employmentboost.com/articles/building-resilience-strategies-for-bouncing-back-from-setbacks-and-challenges-in-your-career/

Campbell, P. (2015, February 3). *5 Ways to Bounce Back From Any Setback.* Psychology Today.

https://www.psychologytoday.com/us/blog/imperfect-spirituality/201502/5-ways-bounce-back-any-setback

Chan, K. (2023, June 16). *5 Types of Adversity and Ways to Overcome Them.* Very Well Mind.

https://www.verywellmind.com/types-of-adversity-and-ways-to-overcome-them-7505840

Cherry, K. (2022, October 6). *10 Ways to Build Resilience.* Very Well Mind.

https://www.verywellmind.com/ways-to-become-more-resilient-2795063

Perez, A. *7 Famous People Who Overcame Adversity.*

https://www.stillunfold.com/people/7-famous-people-who-overcame-adversity#:~:text=7%20Famous%20People%20Who%20Overcame%20Adversity%201%201%29,lost%20her%20arm%20when%20she%20was%2013%20

Perry, E. (2022, January 31). *10 Ways to Overcome Adversity and Thrive During Hard Times.* Better Up.

https://www.betterup.com/blog/how-to-overcome-adversity

Wu, M. (2022, May 11) *35 Quotes From Powerful Leaders to Celebrate Black History Month.* Southern Living.

https://www.southernliving.com/culture/black-history-quotes

Chapter 4

Courageous Acts of Kindness

———— ❋❋ ————

"Kindness gives birth to kindness." ~ Sophocles.

It's no secret that being kind is infectious. In fact, that notion was apparent to Sophocles several centuries ago (confirmed by the quote above). You see, if you're kind to others, it often inspires them to be kind to you and other people, too. In the heart of every courageous leader is a whole load of compassion and kindness waiting to be unleashed upon the world. As we journey into chapter four, we'll explore the power of kindness and compassion in leadership.

Think of a time when someone was nice to you and consider how that made you feel. Personally, I'm able to look back at times in my life and recognize the impact that kindness from others has had on me. We'll get back to that a bit later, but for now, just take a moment and consider how kindness has impacted you. This, itself, can be a truly powerful thing!

From the smallest gestures to the most profound acts, kindness has the remarkable ability to inspire, uplift, and unite. It's the basis of empathy and understanding, and it has the power to bridge divides and heal wounds. In this chapter, we'll dive into the profound impact of kindness and compassion in courageous acts, discovering how simple acts of kindness can ignite a fire within.

We'll begin by exploring the power of kindness and then explore some stories of noted people who have made a positive impact through acts of kindness, from everyday heroes to extraordinary changemakers. Being kind is something that most of us are taught by our parents, so this is not a new concept, but taking note of how powerful and courageous it can be is something that we may overlook. These stories serve as reminders of the profound ripple effect of kindness and the transformative power it holds.

Our exploration doesn't end there. We'll also consider how kindness and compassion have impacted our own lives, reflecting on moments of connection, empathy, and understanding that have shaped our leadership journey. I know that there have been many people in my life who have inspired me through their courageous kindness, and this has shaped who I am today and how I lead others.

As we dive deeper into the heart of compassion, we'll uncover how kindness ignites our courageous fire, fueling our determination to lead with empathy, integrity, and authenticity. We'll explore how acts of kindness not only benefit those around us but also strengthen our own sense of purpose and fulfillment as leaders.

Before we conclude this chapter, I'll share some practical strategies for incorporating compassion into leadership and promoting inclusivity, empathy, and understanding in our organizations and communities. From fostering a culture of kindness to championing diversity and meeting people where they are, we'll review how compassionate leadership can drive positive change and create a more just and equitable world for all.

Some leaders don't know this, but it's true—courageous leadership requires us to be compassionate and kind. Together, let's ignite the flames of empathy and understanding and let our acts of kindness illuminate the path to a brighter, more compassionate future.

The Power of Kindness and Compassion in Courageous Acts

Kindness is more than just a virtue; it's a force for good that has the power to transform lives and communities. While that claim is bold, it's true because it's nice when someone is kind to you. It can inspire, motivate, and empower you because you feel like someone gets you or is at least making an effort to relate to how you feel. In the realm of courageous leadership, kindness and compassion serve as guiding principles, pointing the way to positive change and transformation.

The days of employees being scared of leaders and managers are over because the unapproachable style of leadership is stale—it just doesn't work anymore. At its core, kindness is about extending empathy, understanding, and support to others, even in the face of adversity. It's about recognizing the worth and dignity of every person and treating them with respect and compassion, regardless of differences or challenges they may face.

Business leaders increasingly suggest that if we place kindness at the center of leadership strategies, it leads to success. A compassionate approach is more likely to bring positive results, including better employee performance and loyal employees who are more likely to stay with the organization than look for alternative employment.

Courageous kindness goes beyond simple gestures; it requires a willingness to step out of our comfort zone and take bold action to make a positive impact. Whether it's standing up for someone being treated unfairly, lending a helping hand to those in need, or speaking out against injustice, kindness requires strength, empathy, and conviction. If you want to be a good leader, you must stay connected to your team; therefore, these traits are a must. It's ultimately our job to be courageously kind, and if you model these traits, you'll find that the others in your team do, too.

A simple act of kindness has the power to create ripples that can spread far and wide, touching the lives of countless people in meaningful ways.

Whether it's a smile, a kind word, or a small gesture of support, these acts of kindness have the power to brighten someone's day, lift their spirits, and restore their faith in humanity. If you're doing these things as a leader, you'll notice that you're making an impact.

It's often the small things in life that make the biggest difference!

But the benefits of kindness and compassion extend beyond just those who receive them. Research has shown that showing compassion to others improves connectedness, enhances social interactions, and strengthens communities. If you foster a culture of kindness and empathy as a leader, you should create environments where everyone feels valued, supported, and empowered to thrive.

Being kind and compassionate is a win-win situation. Positive behavior breeds positive behavior, which often cascades through the workplace. Studies show that kindness also has health benefits because people who are kind produce lower levels of stress hormones. It builds connections because it shows you're approachable and others can talk to you with ease.

Leading with compassion means prioritizing the well-being and dignity of others, even in the face of challenges or obstacles. It means actively seeking out opportunities to support and uplift those around us and advocating for policies and practices that promote equity, justice, and inclusion for all.

Leaders must cultivate empathy, humility, and a deep sense of connection with others. They must be willing to listen with openness, acknowledge their own biases and limitations, and embrace diversity and difference as sources of strength and enrichment.

Leaders can also inspire trust, build strong relationships, and create environments where people feel valued, respected, and empowered to contribute their best. It's about embracing the power of kindness and compassion in courageous acts and working together to create a world where empathy, understanding, and inclusion reign supreme.

This is the true impact of embracing kindness and compassion in leadership, and it's often the difference between good leaders and great leaders.

Acts of Kindness: Real Stories

Acts of kindness are completed daily by those around us. When I learn about someone who has or is making a difference through courageous acts of kindness and compassion, I develop a new kind of respect for them. They inspire me!

Let's take a look at some outstanding people who are fanning the flames of kindness and compassion:

LeBron James

Basketball legend LeBron James has used his platform and resources to give back to his community in so many ways. Following his own financial insecurity growing up, LeBron James did something amazing by creating the LeBron James Family Foundation in 2004. The foundation provides community outreach programs and education to impact children and families positively.

Chance the Rapper

Chance the Rapper is not only a talented musician but a philanthropist who is dedicated to making a positive community impact. He has donated millions to fund public schools, mental health services, charities, and youth empowerment programs. Throughout his career, he's made significant donations to Chicago Public Schools of over $4 million.

Oprah Winfrey

Oprah is known for her philanthropic work and countless acts of kindness. She believes that education is the key to freedom and I agree—knowledge is power. Something she's done that's notable is creating the Oprah Winfrey Charitable Foundation, which provides grants to people and organizations in need, focusing on education, wellness initiatives, and empowerment. Oprah pledged to build a school in South Africa during a visit with Nelson Mandela in 2002. Now, that's certainly an act of kindness that benefited so many. Since then, she's contributed so much more, including more than $200 million toward education for girls in South Africa from disadvantaged backgrounds but who are academically gifted.

Maya Angelou

Maya Angelou was a renowned author and poet known for her compassionate spirit and commitment to social justice. She used her writing, speaking engagements, and popularity to advocate for equality and empathy, inspiring others to embrace compassion and kindness toward others in their own lives. There's no doubt that her writing has inspired others and won numerous awards, but it's the impact they had that is truly remarkable—especially her autobiographical works, which offer powerful insights into the evolution of twentieth-century Black women.

The people above highlight the power of kindness and compassion in making a difference in the lives of others, regardless of their fame and fortune. They used the resources they had to make a difference, but it's evident that the power to make a difference lies within every one of us.

If we lead with courage and compassion, we can influence, empower, and uplift those in need and leave a lasting legacy of generosity and empathy. The examples above serve as a reminder that kindness knows no bounds. We all have the potential to make a positive difference in the world.

So, what are you waiting for? It's time to leave your mark on the world.

Reflection Time

To deepen your understanding, it's important to consider the impact kindness and compassion have. Take a moment to reflect on the times in your life when kindness and compassion have made a difference.

Consider the ripple effect of these acts of kindness and how they have impacted your life and the lives of those around you.

1. Think about a time when someone showed you kindness or compassion during a challenging situation. *How did their actions make you feel? How did it impact your outlook on the situation?*

2. Reflect on a time when you extended kindness or compassion to someone else, whether it was a friend, family member, coworker, or stranger. *How did your actions affect the other person? Did you notice any positive changes in their mood or behavior?*

3. Consider the ripple effect of kindness and compassion in your life. *How have small acts of kindness from others influenced your day-to-day interactions and relationships? Have you observed how kindness can spread from one person to another, creating a chain reaction of positivity?*

4. Think about how you can incorporate more kindness and compassion into your daily life, including your role as a leader. *Are there simple gestures you can make to brighten someone else's day or offer support to those in need? How can you lead with courage and empathy in your interactions with others?*

5. Consider the impact of kindness and compassion on your community and society as a whole. *How can acts of kindness contribute to building a more inclusive and compassionate world? What role can you play in promoting kindness and empathy in your community?*

Take some time to note your reflections and consider how you can incorporate more kindness and compassion into your life moving forward.

Remember, even the smallest acts of kindness create positive change in the world around us.

How Kindness and Compassion Ignite Your Courageous Fire

It's time to consider how kindness and compassion fit in with being courageous. They are not merely acts of selflessness; they are also a demonstration of our courage and resilience. When we extend kindness and compassion to others, we uplift their spirits while also igniting the flame of courage within ourselves.

Compassion is actually part of your human nature—most of us are taught it throughout our lives, and it keeps things real. *Just ask yourself, what's the point of worrying about something but doing nothing about it?*

It's a waste of time and energy. The truth is that a compassionate person is brave because they're not going to waste that time and energy. They're brave enough to act and face situations (or pain), and despite this, they're able to take on the responsibility.

Let's explore some of the benefits of kindness and compassion and consider how this ignites your courageous fire:

1. Strengthening empathy – Practicing kindness and compassion requires us to empathize with others and to understand and share their feelings. This empathetic connection fosters a deeper understanding of the challenges and struggles faced by others, motivating us to take courageous action to alleviate their suffering.

2. Overcoming fear – Compassion often requires us to step out of our comfort zone and confront our fears. Whether it's speaking up against injustice, offering support to someone in need, or challenging societal norms, acts of compassion demand courage and conviction. By embracing kindness and compassion, we learn to overcome our fears and stand up for what is right, even in the face of adversity (which we've already discussed in chapter three).

3. Building resilience – Acts of kindness and compassion strengthen our resilience by reinforcing our sense of purpose and interconnectedness. When we recognize the impact that our actions can have on others, we become more resilient in the face of challenges and setbacks. Our courage is fueled by the knowledge that even the smallest acts of kindness can make a meaningful difference in the lives of others.

4. Cultivating courageous leadership – Compassionate leadership requires courage—the courage to lead with integrity, empathy, and authenticity. By embodying kindness and compassion in our leadership roles, we inspire others to do the same and create a culture of empathy, inclusion, and collaboration. Courageous leaders understand that true strength lies in compassion and empathy, and they lead by example, demonstrating the power of kindness to effect positive change.

5. Standing up for justice – Kindness and compassion compel us to stand up for justice and equality, even in the face of opposition. Whether it's advocating for marginalized communities, speaking out against discrimination, or promoting social change, acts of compassion require us to be courageous in our convictions. By aligning our actions with our values, we become changemakers, working toward a more just and compassionate world for all.

We can safely say that kindness and compassion are not just virtues; they are also sources of courage and strength. By embracing kindness and compassion in our lives, we make a positive impact on the lives of others while also igniting the flame of courage within ourselves. This empowers us to stand up for what is right and create a brighter, more compassionate world for future generations.

There's something really refreshing about the power that acts of kindness and compassion provide us with.

Unnoticeable Acts of Kindness

I'm extremely grateful and blessed. So many people have been kind to me throughout my life, and this has positively impacted me. Some acts of kindness aren't as deep as others, but they're still worthwhile.

There are a few things I could've talked about here, but I started to think about acts of kindness that have marked my life. One story stands out to me, not because I recognized it as a genuine act of kindness at the time, but because of its profound impact on both my life and that of my younger brother and parents. Over twenty years ago, in 2004, I faced a decision that reshaped our family dynamics and underscored the deep bonds of brotherhood.

Let me explain. . . .

Growing up as the middle child among three boys, I always felt a strong sense of responsibility toward my siblings, especially my younger brother, who was six years younger than I. Our bond was fortified by the countless hours spent under the care of our grandmother while our mom worked. This closeness took on a new dimension in 2002 when my brother was diagnosed with a rare blood disorder that eventually led to kidney failure (I've told you the story of his passing, but this refers to how we got there). Understanding his daily struggle hooked up to a dialysis machine that both sustained and drained his life force was difficult. He deserved better.

When the possibility of a kidney transplant became a reality, I didn't hesitate. After a few years, the doctors confirmed that my brother's condition had stabilized enough for a transplant, and I was a blood match. What followed was six months of rigorous testing, leading us to a historic moment: We would have the first kidney transplant procedure at Kaiser Permanente San Francisco. The procedure not only represented a technical milestone for the hospital but also a personal journey of sacrifice and hope for us. Don't get me wrong, I didn't see it as a sacrifice, if I'm entirely honest, and I didn't consider the impact it could have on me, but I remember feeling a sense of responsibility to my brother. I would have done anything I could to help turn things around for him. I had to help.

The transplant, performed in December of 2004, granted my brother an additional seven years of life, and for that, I'm grateful. During that time, he lived more fully, albeit under the constant shadow of potential organ rejection, mitigated only by daily medication. While I viewed my decision to donate as a mere fulfillment of duty, my parents and others saw it as an act of immense kindness. To this day, my father reminds me of the "gift of life" I offered to my little brother. Over time, I have come to appreciate their perspective, as what I saw as an obligatory act was indeed a gesture of selfless love.

This experience taught me that sometimes, the line between duty and kindness blurs. We may act out of obligation, but to others, our actions resonate as extraordinary generosity. The procedure and loss of a kidney also left me with heightened sensitivity, a literal change in perception, and enhanced senses of smell and hearing—a reminder of the deep connections between sacrifice, health, and sensory awareness.

Reflecting on this journey underscores a crucial lesson: *What we might dismiss as a necessary act can be a monumental act of kindness to others.* This story of brotherly love, medical challenges, and personal sacrifice captures the essence of how our deepest responsibilities can manifest as our greatest acts of kindness.

How Compassion Is Used in Leadership to Promote Inclusivity

Inclusive leadership is rooted in compassion—the ability to empathize with others, understand their perspectives, and create a sense of belonging for everyone. Compassionate leaders recognize the inherent value and dignity of every person and strive to create environments where everyone feels valued, respected, and included.

A leader who feels determined and committed to expressing compassion and kindness can coordinate their team better, improve team bonds, and increase employee satisfaction. It ignites passion; therefore, compassionate leadership is certainly favorable for all.

You can use compassion to promote inclusivity by:

- Fostering Empathy

    Compassionate leaders prioritize empathy, actively seeking to understand the experiences, perspectives, and needs of their team members. By cultivating a culture of empathy, they create space for open dialogue, collaboration, and understanding, fostering a sense of belonging for people from diverse backgrounds.

- Cultivating Diversity

    Compassionate leaders understand the importance of diversity in fostering innovation, creativity, and resilience. They actively seek out and embrace diverse perspectives, experiences, and ideas, recognizing that diversity is a strength that drives organizational success. By fostering a culture of diversity and inclusion, they create opportunities for people from all backgrounds to thrive and contribute to the organization's success.

- Promoting Equity

    Compassionate leaders are committed to promoting equity and fairness in all aspects of their leadership. They recognize and address systemic biases and inequalities, working to create opportunities for all to succeed. By promoting fairness and equity, they create a level playing field where everyone has the opportunity to reach their full potential, regardless of their background or identity.

- Creating Psychological Safety

  Compassionate leaders prioritize creating environments where team members feel safe to speak up, share their ideas, and take risks. They create psychological safety by fostering trust, openness, and vulnerability, allowing people to express themselves authentically without fear of judgment or reprisal. By creating a safe and inclusive environment, they empower people to bring their full selves to work and contribute their unique talents and perspectives.

- Leading with Authenticity

  Compassionate leaders lead with authenticity, integrity, and humility, modeling inclusive behaviors and values for their team members. They acknowledge their own biases and limitations, actively seek feedback and input from others, and demonstrate a willingness to learn and grow. By leading with authenticity, they inspire trust and confidence in their leadership and create a culture where diversity and inclusion are celebrated and valued.

There's no question that compassion is a powerful tool for promoting inclusivity in leadership. Compassionate leaders foster empathy, cultivate diversity, promote equity, create psychological safety, and lead with authenticity, creating environments where everyone feels valued, respected, and included. By prioritizing compassion in your leadership approach, you can create innovative, successful, and more humane and compassionate organizations.

That's the power of compassion and kindness if you dare to embrace and implement them!

Keep that with you as we head into the next chapter and talk about challenging the status quo.

References

30 Random Acts of Kindness Quotes. Tinkl.co.uk

https://www.twinkl.co.uk/blog/30-kindness-quotes-for-random-acts-of-kindness-day#:~:text=%E2%80%9CCarry%20out%20a%20random%20act,plant.%E2%80%9D%20%2D%20Robert%20Louis%20Stevenson

A Rundown on Chance the Rapper's Inspiring Philanthropy. (2023, September 12).

https://bleumag.com/entertainment/chance-the-rapper-philanthropy/

About Us. Oprah Winfrey Charitable Foundation.

https://www.oprahfoundation.org/about-charity

Allen, S. (2019, August 22). *Sharon Allen OBE on Compassionate and Inclusive Leadership.*

https://www.kingsfund.org.uk/insight-and-analysis/videos/sharon-allen-compassionate-leadership

Bhasin, H. (2023, June 9). *Being a Compassionate Leader – Qualities and Importance.*

https://www.marketing91.com/compassionate-leader/#:~:text=3%20Famous%20Compassionate%20Leaders%201%20Francis%20of%20Assisi%2C,author%20from%20Texas%20who%20wrote%20about%20racial%20equality

Bojanic, N. (2021, November 15). *How Compassion Gives You Courage.*

https://balance.media/compassion-gives-courage-2/#:~:text=However%2C%20compassion%20also%20makes%20courage.%20Acting%20out%20of,when%20we%20do%20we%20feel%20transparent%20and%20free

Courageous Compassion. (2021, July 1). Centre for Compassionate Leadership.

https://www.centerforcompassionateleadership.org/blog/courageous-compassion

Heshmat, S. (2022, December 6). *Kindness and Its Benefits: 5 Ways That Sincere Kindness Can Make Our Lives Better.*

https://www.psychologytoday.com/us/blog/science-choice/202212/kindness-and-its-benefits

Johnston, A. (2017, December 21). *11 Small Acts of Kindness That Changed the World Forever.*

https://theculturetrip.com/europe/articles/10-small-acts-of-kindness-that-changed-the-world

Kratz, J. (2023, November 17). *Leadership is About Inclusion. Here's How to Get it Right.* Forbes.

https://www.forbes.com/sites/juliekratz/2023/11/17/leadership-is-about-inclusion-heres-how-to-get-it-right/

Maya Angelou. National Women's Hall of Fame.

https://www.womenofthehall.org/inductee/maya-angelou/

Paatsch, K. (2022, October 20). Kindness More Often Than Not Takes Courage.

https://www.linkedin.com/pulse/kindness-more-often-than-takes-courage-kylie-paatsch/

Reynolds, T. (2023, February 3). *LeBron James' Off-Court Legacy Complements NBA Success.* NBA.com

https://www.nba.com/news/lebron-james-off-court-legacy-complements-nba-success

Tenney, M. *What is Compassionate and Inclusive Leadership?* Business Leadership Today.

https://businessleadershiptoday.com/what-is-compassionate-and-inclusive-leadership/#:~:text=Compassionate%20and%20inclusive%20leadership%20is,their%20growth%20and%20well%2Dbeing.

Chapter 5

Challenging the Status Quo

"Courage is not the absence of fear, but the triumph over it."
~ Nelson Mandela

Standing up for what you believe in and rebelling against fear takes courage. In a world where conformity often reigns supreme, challenging the status quo takes an extraordinary level of courage mixed with a little conviction. It means daring to question long-held beliefs, societal norms, and institutionalized practices in pursuit of a better, more just world. In this chapter, we'll delve into the essence of courageous fire, exploring what it means to challenge the status quo and the courage required to do so.

At its core, challenging the status quo is about refusing to accept things as they are simply because they've always been that way. It's about recognizing injustice, inequality, and oppression and refusing to turn a blind eye. It's about speaking truth to power and advocating for change, even in the face of resistance and adversity.

Yet, while challenging the status quo may sound straightforward, it isn't an easy thing to do. It requires stepping outside of our comfort zone, risking social ostracism, and facing backlash from those who benefit from the existing order. It means confronting deeply ingrained biases and systemic injustices that have perpetuated inequality for generations.

But isn't this what we should be doing as leaders anyway?

Absolutely! Part of leading with your courageous fire means challenging the norms and standing up for what's right. The thing is, no one teaches us how to do this and how to become more courageous, which means we're not necessarily equipped to challenge the status quo—it's not always something we feel confident doing. Being more courageous is a skill that most leaders develop as they become more experienced (and, with it, bolder).

You're probably wondering why it's so important. Well, despite the challenges, history has shown us time and again that those who dare to challenge the status quo bring about the greatest positive change. From civil rights leaders who fought against racial segregation to suffragettes who campaigned for women's right to vote, courageous people and movements have reshaped the course of history all over the world by challenging entrenched norms and injustices. Only now, *it's not their fight, it's yours. We can't stop now!*

In this chapter, we'll explore why it's difficult to challenge the status quo, examining the psychological, social, and institutional barriers that stand in the way of progress. We'll also draw inspiration from historical figures and movements that have defied the odds to bring about positive change, reminding us that no obstacle is insurmountable when fueled by the fire of courage.

It's time to discover the transformative power of challenging the status quo, as standing up for the things we believe in is empowering. We just have to find the courage within ourselves to do so, even when the odds seem stacked against us.

Challenging the Norms

Courage pushes us to challenge the norms and stand up for what is right, even in the face of adversity. Your courage plays an indispensable role in challenging the status quo and driving progress forward. Courageous acts have a huge impact when it comes to reshaping societal norms and institutions, while both complacency and inaction have consequences.

When we stand up for something we believe in, it means something to us, and therefore, it ignites our courage. At its core, challenging the norms requires a willingness to confront your beliefs, values, and practices that perpetuate injustice, inequality, and oppression. It demands the courage to question authority, challenge prevailing narratives, and advocate for marginalized voices to be heard. Whether it's speaking out against systemic racism, advocating for equality, or fighting for environmental justice, courageous people play a pivotal role in challenging the status quo and driving social change.

Like everything in life, the decision to challenge the norms is not without its risks. It can be a scary thing because it requires us to step outside of our comfort zone, risking our reputation, livelihood, and even personal safety in pursuit of justice and equality. Standing up against powerful institutions, interests, and societal norms can invite backlash, condemnation, and even persecution. It's precisely these moments of adversity that courage shines at its brightest, inspiring others to join the fight for a better world.

The consequences of complacency and inaction can be dire. Just imagine if nobody had stood up against slavery, human rights, or women's right to vote. There is still a fight for equality and equity going on today—although things are better, it's certainly not perfect, with so much more room for growth. It's hard to imagine a world in which there has been no progress at all, *isn't it?*

When people fail to challenge the status quo, injustice and inequities continue to thrive unchecked. Oppressive systems remain unchallenged, marginalized communities continue to suffer, and progress stagnates. As the saying goes, "The only thing necessary for the triumph of evil is for good men to do nothing." (Rentoul, 2017). Therefore, it's incumbent upon each of us to summon the courage to challenge the norms and stand up for what is right for the sake of ourselves and future generations.

As leaders, we're in charge of driving and leaving change, and therefore, we could say that challenging the status quo is, in fact, our responsibility.

Why Is It Difficult to Challenge the Status Quo?

Challenging the status quo is inherently difficult due to a multitude of factors that reinforce the existing norms and power structures within society. We spend so much time following these structures that it's sometimes difficult to see what's wrong with them.

Let's look at some reasons why challenging the status quo isn't always easy:

- Fear of reprisal – One of the most significant barriers to challenging the status quo is the fear of reprisal or backlash from those in power. Speaking out against established norms or institutions can invite retaliation, ostracism, or even physical harm, particularly for marginalized individuals or those with less social or economic capital.

- Social conformity – Human beings are inherently social creatures, and we have a natural inclination to conform to the beliefs, values, and behaviors of the groups to which we belong. Challenging the status quo often means going against the grain and risking social rejection or alienation from peers, family members, or colleagues.

- Institutional resistance – Institutions and systems of power have a vested interest in maintaining the status quo, as it serves to reinforce their authority and privilege. They may employ various tactics to resist change, including co-opting dissent, marginalizing dissenters, or employing legal and institutional barriers to suppress opposition.

- Psychological barriers – Challenging the status quo can evoke feelings of uncertainty, self-doubt, and cognitive dissonance as individuals grapple with the conflicting demands of their beliefs and the prevailing norms. Fear of failure, rejection, or ridicule may also undermine individuals' confidence in their ability to effect change.

- Lack of resources – Effecting meaningful change often requires resources such as time, money, expertise, and social networks. People from marginalized or underprivileged backgrounds may lack access to these resources, making it challenging for them to challenge the status quo effectively.

- Cultural conditioning – Societal norms and cultural values shape our perceptions of what is acceptable and permissible behavior. People may internalize these norms from a young age, making it difficult to question or challenge them later in life.

I mentioned earlier that it can be scary to challenge the status quo, and many people find themselves afraid to do this. I have to be honest; challenging the status quo entails a degree of risk, as there is no guarantee of success. Fear of failure can paralyze people, preventing them from taking action or speaking out for fear of being unable to effect meaningful change. That's why challenging and overcoming these things and challenging the status quo are, in fact, courageous acts in themselves.

Challenging the status quo may subject people to social stigma or ridicule from others who are invested in maintaining the existing norms. Fear of social ostracism or backlash can deter others from challenging it, even when they believe it is morally or ethically wrong. That's because the status quo often provides us with a sense of comfort, familiarity, and security, even when it is unjust or inequitable. Challenging this disrupts this sense of stability, leading people to fear the unknown consequences of change. But we have to work through the fear—we can't let it stop us from progress!

It didn't take me long to realize that those who show such courage and benefit from challenging the status quo often hold positions of power and influence within society. This means confronting power structures and risking reprisal from those in authority, creating a sense of powerlessness and vulnerability among dissenters.

Let's be honest: Challenging the status quo can be a lonely and isolating endeavor, particularly if we lack support from peers, allies, or communities. Without a network of support, it's not uncommon for people to feel overwhelmed or discouraged from challenging the prevailing norms. I get this, as there are times when I've felt this way, too. While challenging the status quo is fraught with difficulties and obstacles, it's essential for progress and social change.

If we understand the barriers to challenging the status quo and acknowledge our fears, we can begin to overcome them and summon the courage to stand up for what is right.

Reflection Time

Take some time to think about the "status quo" in your life or society that impacts you.

- What would you personally like to challenge the "status quo" of?

- Consider norms, practices, or systems that you believe are unjust, inequitable, or in need of change.

- Write down your thoughts and feelings about why you feel compelled to challenge this aspect of the status quo and what steps you can take to advocate for change.

- Remember, even small acts of resistance and advocacy can contribute to meaningful progress and social transformation.

They Challenged the Status Quo!

By suggesting you challenge the status quo, I'm not asking you to do something new or something that's never been done before. While some challenges will be unique and new, challenging the status quo is something people have been doing for centuries. There are so many people in the world who've challenged this and won. What I mean by this is that they've taken action, and as a result, they've made a difference and have brought about positive change despite it being scary.

To strengthen your knowledge, let's take a look at some examples of those people:

- Leaders like Martin Luther King, Jr., Rosa Parks, and Malcolm X challenged the status quo by organizing peaceful protests, boycotts, and acts of civil disobedience to demand an end to racial segregation and discrimination. Their courageous actions challenged entrenched systems of oppression and brought about significant legislative and social change.

- Figures like Harriet Tubman, Frederick Douglass, and Sojourner Truth challenged the status quo by speaking out against the institution of slavery and actively working to liberate enslaved individuals through the Underground Railroad and other means. Their advocacy helped shift public opinion and ultimately led to the abolition of slavery in the United States.

- Leaders like Susan B. Anthony, Elizabeth Cady Stanton, and Ida B. Wells challenged the status quo by advocating for women's right to vote through public speaking, writing, and organizing suffrage campaigns. Despite facing opposition and resistance, their persistent efforts contributed to the eventual passage of the Nineteenth Amendment, granting women the right to vote.

- Orville and Wilbur Wright challenged the status quo by daring to pursue their dream of powered flight at a time when conventional wisdom held that human flight was impossible. Through meticulous experimentation and innovation, they defied skeptics and critics to achieve the first successful powered flight, revolutionizing transportation and opening new possibilities for human exploration and discovery.

- Inventors and entrepreneurs challenged the status quo by introducing groundbreaking innovations in agriculture, industry, and business during the Industrial Revolution. Figures like George Washington Carver and Madam C.J. Walker challenged prevailing norms and stereotypes, contributing to advancements in science, technology, and economic opportunity.

- Innovators like Garrett Morgan and Lonnie Johnson challenged the status quo by inventing new technologies that transformed daily life and industry. Morgan's invention of the traffic signal and Johnson's creation of the Super Soaker water gun challenged conventional thinking and opened new frontiers in safety and entertainment.

These examples illustrate how courageous people and movements challenged the status quo by confronting entrenched systems of inequality, discrimination, and limitation, inspiring others to envision and create a more just, equitable, and inclusive world. There's no reason why you can't channel your courageous fire to create your legacy, to influence and drive positive change.

Challenging the Status Quo: A Recurring Theme in My Life

This is just a short snippet of my own experience with the status quo, as challenging the status quo has been a recurring theme throughout my life, and it's one that holds particular significance. As I reflect on my experiences navigating the complexities of challenging norms, I'm drawn to discussing those that relate to my career, especially within the context of my work in the public school system.

In my role(s), I've witnessed firsthand the evolution of laws and regulations governing and impacting education. Over the years, the California education code has ballooned from 24 articles in 1943 to a staggering 1264 articles in 2023. How can anyone follow this outlandish plethora of "rules"? This proliferation of rules and regulations often presents challenges and unintended consequences, particularly when compliance conflicts with what is deemed right or best for students.

Navigating these challenges requires critical thinking and a willingness to challenge the status quo. It involves transforming compliance into a deeper understanding of our responsibilities and obligations to those we serve. As leaders, it's imperative that we encourage and foster a culture of critical thinking among our teams, empowering them to question existing norms and policies.

While laws and regulations are typically created with positive intent, they don't always result in the desired outcomes. This discrepancy can have unintended consequences for students and educators alike, so there are times when I've had to seemingly "go with my gut." I'm pointing out that there are many occasions in our lives when we must summon the courage to speak up, to challenge the status quo, and to advocate for what we believe is right—because it's the right thing to do. Compliance is not my goal; it's supporting people and students.

Now that we've talked about my personal experiences, let's talk about the positives because challenging the status quo certainly has its benefits.

Status Quo: The Benefits

Let's take some time to talk about the benefits of challenging the status quo. When challenging the status quo, it's essential to consider various aspects and implications beyond the immediate change sought. When you're challenging the status quo, it takes time—so you have to be patient. It often involves advocating for greater social justice and equity by addressing systemic inequalities and biases that perpetuate discrimination and marginalization based on factors such as race, gender, socioeconomic status, and more.

Doing this can also lead to significant cultural transformations by challenging outdated norms, values, and practices that no longer serve the needs or reflect the values of a changing society. This can include promoting diversity, inclusion, and cultural acceptance. Challenging the status quo can have profound economic implications by disrupting existing industries, business models, and power structures. It may involve advocating for fair wages, workers' rights, environmental sustainability, or redistributive policies to address economic disparities.

Challenging the status quo often intersects with political change by challenging existing power dynamics, policies, and governance structures. This can involve advocating for policy reforms, electoral changes, or grassroots movements aimed at democratizing decision-making processes and amplifying marginalized voices. This can also include advocating for environmental sustainability and addressing pressing issues such as climate change, pollution, resource depletion, and habitat destruction. This may involve promoting renewable energy, conservation efforts, and sustainable practices in various sectors.

Education involves reimagining traditional educational systems and practices to better meet the needs of diverse learners in the twenty-first century. This is something I can vouch for personally, as I work in education, and it's something I'm extremely passionate about. There have been many times I've had to challenge the status quo, and it means that positive improvements have been made. Common changes in education can include promoting innovative teaching methods, equitable access to quality education, and addressing systemic barriers to learning.

Challenging the status quo often involves harnessing the power of technology to drive innovation and positive change in various fields such as healthcare, transportation, communication, and beyond. This may involve advocating for digital inclusion and responsible tech development. Tech is growing and developing constantly, and it's something that we've all had to learn to adapt to.

In healthcare, this involves advocating for equitable access to healthcare services, addressing systemic health disparities, and promoting holistic approaches to health and well-being. This can include mental health awareness, preventive care, and destigmatizing healthcare access.

On a global scale, challenging the status quo involves fostering international cooperation and solidarity to address pressing challenges such as poverty, conflict, human rights abuses, and humanitarian crises. This may involve promoting diplomacy, peacebuilding efforts, and sustainable development goals. Challenging the status quo also involves empowering people to advocate for change in their own lives and communities. This can include promoting self-awareness, critical thinking, activism, and civic engagement to effect positive change at the grassroots level.

Tackling Resistance

If you're going to drive any type of change, you're going to face resistance. That's normal, but you shouldn't let it stop you. So, before we wrap up the chapter, I wanted to share some advice to help you overcome this:

1. Build a strong coalition - Don't go it alone. Collaborate with like-minded people, organizations, or communities to amplify your message and demonstrate widespread support for your cause.

2. Educate and inform – Knowledge is power. Arm yourself with facts, statistics, and evidence to educate others about the issues and dispel misinformation or misconceptions.

3. Engage in dialogue – Foster open and respectful conversations with those who may oppose your efforts. Listen to their concerns, address their questions, and seek common ground to build understanding and consensus.

4. Lead by example – Actions speak louder than words. Demonstrate your commitment to change through your integrity, consistency, and determination. Be a role model for others to follow.

5. Stay resilient – Challenging the status quo can be tough, and setbacks are inevitable. Stay resilient in the face of adversity, learn from challenges, and adapt your strategies as needed while staying focused on your goals.

6. Appeal to shared values – Find common ground by appealing to shared values or principles. Frame your message in terms that resonate with others' deeply held beliefs, making it easier for them to support your cause.

7. Celebrate successes - Don't forget to acknowledge and celebrate victories, no matter how small. Recognizing progress boosts morale and motivates continued action.

By following these seven tips, you can effectively navigate resistance and advance positive change, even when faced with significant opposition. Just remember, challenging the status quo is a marathon, not a sprint, so it's important that you stay committed and keep pushing forward.

As we navigate the complexities of challenging the status quo, we unearth invaluable lessons that lie at the very heart of courageous leadership. You've explored people and movements that dared to defy convention and uncovered the transformative power of courage, determination, and conviction. These trailblazers and changemakers all share a common trait: the audacity to challenge the status quo.

The question is, are you ready to be audacious? Let your courageous fire drive you.

As we've discovered, courage is not the absence of fear but the willingness to act in spite of it. It's about standing up for what is right, even when it's unpopular or risky. Courageous leaders understand that progress requires pushing boundaries, questioning norms, and embracing change. They are guided by a sense of purpose and a commitment to justice, equality, and innovation.

This is about inspiring others to foster a culture of empowerment, creativity, and growth. They understand true leadership is not about maintaining the status quo but driving positive change and creating a better future for all.

As we reflect on these key insights, we recognize there's so much more to courageous fire in leadership than meets the eye. It's not just about making bold decisions or taking risks; it's about embodying integrity, empathy, and resilience in the face of adversity. It's about leading with conviction and compassion, even when the path is uncertain.

Next, we'll explore how courageous fire manifests in our relationships, driving us to forge deeper connections, foster empathy, and cultivate trust. Let's use our courage to build stronger, more meaningful relationships.

References

Belegisanin, I. (2020, April 21) *78 Events Across 100 Years That Completely Changed the World.*

https://www.emlii.com/78-events-across-100-years-that-completely-changed-the-world/

Black Inventors Who Changed Society. Lee & Hayes.

https://www.leehayes.com/press-releases/38/black-inventors-who-changed-society

Black Leaders Provide Groundbreaking Inventions, Transformative Leadership Throughout History. (2024, January 20). SME.

https://www.sme.org/sme-blog/posts/black-leaders-provide-groundbreaking-inventions-transformative-leadership-throughout-history/

Bradshaw, F. (2019, April 4). *How to Challenge the Status Quo.* Mindtools.

https://www.mindtools.com/blog/challenge-status-quo-successfully/

Challenging the Status Quo. (2023, October 29). Director Prep.

https://savvy.directorprep.com/blog/challenging-the-status-quo

Civil Rights Movement. (2024, May 14). History.com

https://www.history.com/topics/black-history/civil-rights-movement

Differentiate Yourself as a Leader: 4 Ways to Challenge the Status Quo. (2024, June 3).

https://www.linkedin.com/business/learning/blog/leadership-and-management/challenge-the-status-quo-and-differentiate-as-a-leader#:~:text=Maybe%20the%20biggest%20reason%20why,place%20for%20a%20long%20time.

Field, C T. (2021, February 15). *OLD-AGE JUSTICE AND BLACK FEMINIST HISTORY: SOJOURNER TRUTH'S AND HARRIET TUBMAN'S INTERSECTIONAL LEGACIES.*

https://wgs.as.virginia.edu/news/story/old-age-justice-and-black-feminist-history-sojourner-truth%E2%80%99s-and-harriet-tubman%E2%80%99s

From Outsiders to Leaders: Harriet Tubman and Frederick Douglass. (2023, June 13). Thirteen.org.

https://www.thirteen.org/blog-post/outsiders-leaders-harriet-tubman-and-frederick-douglass/

Goodreads. (2023, September 24). *Nelson Mandela Quotes.*

https://www.goodreads.com/quotes/11003936-courage-is-not-the-absence-of-fear-but-the-triumph

Guide to Challenging the Status Quo at Work (With Tips). (2022, June 25). Indeed.

https://www.indeed.com/career-advice/career-development/challenging-the-status-quo

Llopis, G. (2017, August 12). *5 Reasons Leaders Are Afraid to Challenge The Status Quo.*

https://www.forbes.com/sites/glennllopis/2017/08/12/5-reasons-leaders-are-afraid-to-challenge-the-status-quo/

Rentoul J. (2017, August 26). *The Top 10: Misattributed Quotations.*

https://www.independent.co.uk/voices/the-top-10-misattributed-quotations-a7910361.html

Resistance to Change: 7 Causes & How to Overcome Them (2024). What Fix.

https://whatfix.com/blog/causes-of-resistance-to-change/

Spring, Kealy. (2021, October 27). *Overcoming Resistance to Change Within Your Organization.* Better Up.

https://www.betterup.com/blog/resistance-to-change

Woman Suffrage and the 19th Amendment. (2021, June 2). Archives.gov

https://www.archives.gov/education/lessons/woman-suffrage

Chapter 6

Courageous Fire in Relationships

"A genuine leader is not a searcher for consensus but a molder of consensus." ~ Martin Luther King, Jr.

It's true, as a leader, you don't need consensus (although it's *nice* or sometimes *easier* to have it). It's a leader's responsibility to make decisions (with or without consensus) and still build and maintain positive relationships with others. I'm a firm believer in what Martin Luther King, Jr. says above: A leader does not search for consensus; they mold it. To allow a leader to mold this, they need courage because they must make courageous decisions, even when others don't agree.

A leader has many relationships in their life that they need to maintain. They must maintain their personal relationships and their relationships with their team, which means they have to be able to communicate well and ensure everyone is on the same page. There are many times I've had to make unpopular decisions in my line of work, but I always have a sense of confidence—it's always for the greater good. To act takes courage, and courage is part of everything a leader does, but to do this effectively, they need to use their courageous fire to overcome the fear.

Navigating relationships (both personally and professionally) is both an art and a science. From professional collaborations to personal connections, the quality of our relationships can impact our ability to lead effectively. In this chapter, we'll dive into the complex dynamics of relationships (again, both personally and professionally), exploring how courage ignites the flames of the *three C's*: connection, communication, and collaboration.

Courage plays a vital role in every aspect of our relationships. It requires a person to have the bravery to speak up, to listen with empathy, and to navigate difficult conversations with grace and authenticity. As leaders, our ability to cultivate courageous relationships sets the foundation for trust, respect, and mutual understanding.

Throughout this chapter, we'll explore how courage manifests in our interactions with others, from the boardroom to the breakroom and in our homes and communities. We'll examine the importance of effective communication, vulnerability, and trust in building strong and resilient relationships. Drawing on insights from psychology, leadership theory, and real-world examples, we'll uncover strategies for fostering courageous relationships that empower individuals and teams to thrive.

As leaders, we have the opportunity—and the responsibility—to cultivate environments where courage flourishes, authenticity is valued, and relationships are nurtured with care. It's time to explore the power of courageous fire in relationships and discover how it shapes our hearts and souls both professionally and personally.

Navigating Relationships in Life

Navigating relationships in life is an essential skill for leaders aiming to foster positive connections, both personally and professionally. We can't possibly read other people's minds, so to avoid misunderstandings, we need positive communication. It's a must. This is something that, for the most part, we do subconsciously, but learning to navigate the relationships we have in life can make them stronger. It's something we can get better at, and it will improve all aspects of our lives.

We all want better relationships. That often means listening well, apologizing when we make mistakes, talking about how we feel, and asking others how they feel while recognizing and respecting differences in beliefs, opinions, values, and personalities. These things help to build and maintain healthy relationships, which is exactly what we're aiming for.

Building and maintaining healthy relationships can greatly influence our long-term success and fulfillment. So, let's explore some key strategies for navigating relationships effectively:

- Communication

  Effective communication is the cornerstone of any successful relationship. Leaders should prioritize clear, open, and honest communication to establish trust and understanding with others. Active listening, empathy, and clarity in expressing thoughts and feelings are crucial components of effective communication.

- Empathy

  Understanding and empathizing with others' perspectives and emotions is vital for building strong relationships. Leaders should strive to see situations from others' viewpoints, validate their feelings, and respond with compassion and understanding. Empathy fosters connection, trust, and mutual respect in relationships.

- Boundaries

  Setting and respecting boundaries is essential for healthy relationships. Leaders should establish clear boundaries to define expectations, responsibilities, and limits in their interactions with others. Respecting others' boundaries and communicating our own boundaries helps maintain mutual respect and harmony in relationships.

- Conflict Resolution

  Conflict is inevitable in any relationship, but how it's managed can determine the strength and longevity of the relationship. Leaders should approach conflicts constructively, seeking mutual understanding, compromise, and resolution. Effective conflict resolution involves active listening, empathy, and a willingness to find mutually beneficial solutions.

- Building Trust

  Trust is the foundation of any meaningful relationship. Leaders should demonstrate integrity, reliability, and authenticity to earn the trust of others. Consistency in actions, transparency in communication, and honoring commitments are essential for building and maintaining trust in relationships.

- Cultivating Positivity

  Fostering positivity and appreciation in relationships can strengthen connections and enhance overall well-being. Leaders should cultivate an environment of positivity, appreciation, and gratitude by acknowledging others' contributions, celebrating achievements, and expressing genuine care and support.

- Adaptability

  Relationships evolve over time, and leaders should be adaptable and flexible in navigating these changes. Being open to feedback, adjusting expectations, and embracing change can help maintain healthy and resilient relationships amidst life's transitions and challenges.

If you prioritize effective communication, empathy, boundaries, conflict resolution, trust building, positivity, and adaptability, you can navigate relationships in life with grace, integrity, and authenticity, fostering meaningful connections and promoting mutual growth and success.

How Courage Plays a Vital Role in Personal Relationships

Have you ever taken a moment to consider the role courage plays in your personal relationships?

Probably more than you first realize.

You see, courage plays a vital role in personal relationships by empowering us to navigate vulnerability, express authenticity, and cultivate deeper connections with others. It can give you confidence and strengthen your relationships, so there's no doubt that courage has the power to influence them.

True intimacy and connection require vulnerability—the willingness to expose our authentic selves, including fears, insecurities, and emotions. The truth is, without these things, we wouldn't need courage because it takes courage to be vulnerable and to share our innermost thoughts and feelings with another person, risking rejection or judgment. However, there is something really refreshing and empowering about sharing those things. It's through vulnerability that trust and intimacy are built, allowing us to form deeper, more meaningful connections with others.

Courage also enables us to show up authentically in our relationships without pretense or feeling the need to mask our true selves. Being true to yourself and expressing genuine thoughts, feelings, and values fosters authenticity in relationships, creating a foundation of trust and mutual respect. Authenticity just breeds further authenticity, as it invites others to do the same, leading to more authentic and fulfilling connections.

As we've been discussing so far, courage involves taking risks, which can also mean stepping outside your comfort zone, facing uncertainty, and embracing the unknown. In personal relationships, this might mean initiating difficult conversations, expressing unpopular opinions, or making oneself emotionally vulnerable. Taking such risks can lead to growth, deeper understanding, and strengthened bonds with others. It's normal for us not to see eye to eye with someone all the time, and it takes courage to talk through those situations. Just imagine if we didn't do this, and relationships broke down every time we disagreed with another person. We'd never build long-lasting relationships with anyone.

Courage is needed to set and enforce boundaries in personal relationships. Asserting your needs, values, and limits while respecting those of others is an important aspect of relationship building. Setting boundaries requires courage because it may involve confronting conflict, disappointing others, or risking the loss of the relationship. However, healthy boundaries are essential for maintaining mutual respect, safety, and well-being in relationships.

Personal relationships inevitably evolve over time, and courage is needed to embrace these changes and navigate transitions together. Whether it's adapting to new circumstances, supporting each other through challenges, or letting go of outdated dynamics, courage enables individuals to navigate change with resilience, openness, and compassion.

Courage is required to practice forgiveness and compassion in personal relationships—letting go of resentment, offering grace, and extending empathy to oneself and others. Forgiveness and compassion require strength and courage because they involve vulnerability, humility, and a willingness to let go of grievances in favor of healing and reconciliation.

We can't deny that courage plays a vital role in personal relationships by empowering people to embrace vulnerability, authenticity, risk-taking, boundary-setting, change, forgiveness, and compassion. If you cultivate courage in your relationships, you can all begin to foster deeper connections, mutual understanding, and emotional intimacy, leading to more fulfilling and meaningful interpersonal connections.

That's what we all want, right?

Courageous Relationships: Leading through Difficult Situations

For many people, a journey in education often starts with a passion for learning and a desire to make a difference in the lives of students. Yet, as we progress into leadership roles, we come to realize that our responsibilities extend far beyond the classroom—especially as we take on more administrative duties. We become the stewards of conflict, tasked with guiding our teams through some difficult times. Conflict often seems to be at the center of it all.

My own journey into education administration began as a special education administrator, then in human resources, where I honed my skills in leading people and resolving conflicts. Over the past twenty years, I've navigated countless challenging situations, each teaching me valuable lessons about communication, empathy, and trust.

At the heart of courageous fire in relationships lies the ability to communicate effectively, empathize with others, and resolve conflicts without resorting to blame. Blaming others isn't something I value. I solve problems, and I always hold my hands up and admit the truth if something seems wrong to me. I've learned that it's never about blame but building trust over time so that when you speak, your words carry weight and authenticity.

I have to be completely honest here and tell you that one of the toughest aspects of my role has been the necessity to terminate employees. Despite the discomfort of these situations, I've always remained committed to treating each person with dignity and respect. Time and time again, I was humbled by the gratitude expressed by those leaving the organization. It felt odd, but it was also a powerful reminder that compassion and empathy can soften even the harshest of blows. I've always treated others with dignity and respect, so they treated me the same way despite the circumstances.

Through these experiences, I've come to understand that people are not defined by their mistakes but by how they respond to them. This doesn't make them bad people, even if their actions have been unacceptable, but as leaders, it's our responsibility to hold firm to our boundaries while still extending empathy and understanding. Courageous fire in relationships means standing firm in our convictions while also extending a hand of compassion to those in need.

I'm proud to say that many of those I've had to part ways with have thanked me for my approach, acknowledging the compassion and empathy I brought to the table. It's a testament to the power of courageous leadership and the transformative impact it can have on those we lead. I believe my human resources style and people-first approach helped with my ability to handle the most complex situations.

The journey of leadership is complex, but let us remember that conflict is not necessarily the enemy but rather an opportunity for growth and learning. If we move forward with courage and compassion, we can navigate even the most challenging of situations, emerging stronger and more resilient than before.

Having courageous fire in relationships is at the center of making things better in life, but it's something that you, over time, have to build up to by embracing the strategies to follow soon in this chapter.

Just remember that when there's conflict, there's always a better way to deal with it.

Reflection Time

Take a moment to reflect on the relationships in your life, both personal and professional.

Then, consider the following questions to assess the level of courage present in your relationships:

1. Are you willing to be vulnerable and authentic with the people in your life?

2. Do you share your true thoughts, feelings, and experiences openly, even if it feels uncomfortable or risky?

3. Do you show up as your genuine self in your relationships, or do you wear masks or hide parts of yourself to fit in or avoid conflict?

4. Are you willing to take risks in your relationships, such as initiating difficult conversations, expressing unpopular opinions, or making yourself emotionally vulnerable?

5. Do you assert your needs, values, and limits in your relationships and respect the boundaries of others?

6. Are you willing to have honest conversations about boundaries and expectations?

7. How do you navigate change and transitions in your relationships?

8. Are you open to growth and evolution, or do you resist change and cling to familiar patterns?

9. How do you handle conflicts, misunderstandings, and hurts in your relationships?

10. Are you able to offer forgiveness and extend compassion to yourself and others?

Reflecting on these questions can help you assess the level of courage present in your relationships and identify areas for growth and development.

Remember that cultivating courage in your relationships is an ongoing journey, and small steps toward vulnerability, authenticity, risk-taking, boundary-setting, change, forgiveness, and compassion can lead to deeper connections and more fulfilling relationships.

Your courageous fire keeps you committed to the relationships in your life!

Courageous Leadership: Communication, Vulnerability, and Trust

I pride myself on being a courageous leader, and a key component of keeping the flame of my courageous fire roaring is my ability to communicate well with others. Communicating isn't simply about talking to others but also about listening (well). Effective communication, vulnerability, and trust are essential elements of courageous relationships, so in this section, we'll explore how these components contribute to fostering deeper connections and creating environments of mutual respect and understanding.

Communication is at the heart of any relationship, transcending mere exchange of words to encompass a range of verbal and nonverbal cues that convey emotions, intentions, and aspirations. It's through open, honest, and empathetic communication that we form connections, resolve conflicts, and navigate the complexities of human interaction with grace and integrity.

Yet, the path to courageous communication is fraught with challenges due to misunderstandings, biases, and barriers that hinder authentic connection and inhibit vulnerability. It's important to address the obstacles, uncover strategies and insights to overcome them, and cultivate a culture of transparency, empathy, and active listening in our relationships.

This makes me think: *How many people in the world stop talking to one another as a result of miscommunication and misunderstandings?* Maybe there's a way we can change that by communicating more compassionately and effectively.

Vulnerability is often misconstrued as a sign of weakness—at least, this is what I was always taught. However, it's emerged as a catalyst for genuine connection and growth in courageous relationships. It's the courage to show up authentically, to share our fears, insecurities, and aspirations with others, and to embrace the discomfort of uncertainty and imperfection that propels us toward deeper understanding and intimacy.

It certainly takes a brave person to disclose those things! They ultimately show others our human side (yes, leaders are human too).

Trust is the keystone of all meaningful relationships, and this is nurtured through consistent and transparent communication, empathetic listening, and the courageous act of honoring commitments and demonstrating reliability. It's important to explore the dynamics of trust building, uncovering the delicate balance between vulnerability and accountability that underpins its foundation.

As courageous leaders, we recognize that our ability to communicate effectively, embrace vulnerability, and foster trust is vital to our endeavors' success and instrumental in shaping a culture of inclusivity, innovation, and collaboration. Through reflection, dialogue, and intentional practice, we can transform and cultivate the courageous relationships that inspire, empower, and uplift those around us.

Let's talk about how you can do this!

Communication in Relationships

Communication forms the foundation of all successful relationships, whether personal or professional. In courageous relationships, communication goes beyond surface-level interactions and delves into meaningful dialogue that fosters growth and connection.

Let's reflect on the four key elements of effective communication in courageous relationships:

- Openness and honesty – Courageous communication involves being open and honest with oneself and others. It means expressing thoughts, feelings, and concerns authentically, even if they are uncomfortable or difficult to discuss.

- Active listening – Listening is a crucial aspect of communication in courageous relationships. It involves fully engaging with others, seeking to understand their perspectives, and validating their experiences without judgment or interruption.

- Empathy and understanding – Courageous communication requires empathy and understanding toward others' thoughts, feelings, and experiences. It involves acknowledging and validating their emotions, even if they differ from your own.

- Clarity and transparency – Clear and transparent communication helps avoid misunderstandings and promotes trust in relationships. It involves expressing oneself clearly and directly, avoiding ambiguity or mixed messages.

Strategies for Improving Communication

Building courageous relationships requires intentional effort and the adoption of strategies to improve communication. There are some practical steps you can take to enhance communication in your relationships, so let's look at some of those:

- Practice active listening – Make a conscious effort to listen actively to others without interrupting or formulating responses in your mind. Show empathy and understanding by paraphrasing what the speaker has said and reflecting on their emotions.

- Be vulnerable – Embrace vulnerability by sharing your thoughts, feelings, and experiences openly with others. Vulnerability fosters trust and connection in relationships and encourages reciprocal sharing from others.

- Seek feedback – Invite feedback from others about your communication style and how it impacts them. Be open to constructive criticism and use it as an opportunity for self-improvement and growth.

- Clarify expectations – Clearly communicate your expectations and boundaries in relationships and encourage others to do the same. Establishing clear communication norms helps prevent misunderstandings and promotes mutual respect.

- Practice empathy – Put yourself in the shoes of others and try to understand their perspectives and experiences. Show empathy and compassion toward their feelings and validate their emotions, even if you disagree with their viewpoints.

- Resolve conflicts constructively – Approach conflicts in relationships with a focus on finding mutually beneficial solutions rather than assigning blame or winning arguments. Practice active listening, empathy, and problem-solving skills to resolve conflicts peacefully.

By incorporating these strategies into your communication practices, you can enhance the quality of your relationships and foster a culture of openness, trust, and collaboration.

Let's talk about the importance of vulnerability in courageous relationships and discuss how embracing vulnerability can deepen connections and foster authenticity.

Embracing Vulnerability in Courageous Relationships

Vulnerability is often misunderstood as weakness, but in reality, it's a cornerstone of courage and authenticity in relationships. I, for one, most certainly believed it was a weakness, so if you think that, you're not the only one. What I've come to learn is that when you allow yourself to be vulnerable with others, you open yourself up to deeper connections and genuine intimacy.

Being vulnerable isn't a weakness; it means allowing yourself to be seen, flaws and all, without fear of judgment or rejection. It requires honesty, transparency, and a willingness to share your true thoughts, feelings, and experiences with others. People appreciate seeing the real you, but some of us spend our time trying to be something we think others *want* us to be rather than being who we are, making us unauthentic. It's fake, and trust me, other people can see through this!

In courageous relationships, vulnerability is embraced as a strength rather than a weakness. It's the foundation upon which trust is built, and authentic connections are formed. When you're vulnerable with others, you invite them to do the same, creating a safe space for open and honest communication. You're basically telling them, *It's okay to be you because being you is enough.* That's a powerful thing. It builds confidence quickly!

Embracing vulnerability in relationships requires courage and self-awareness. It means stepping outside of your comfort zone and taking risks (like we've already discussed in this chapter), knowing that the rewards of deeper connections and greater intimacy are worth the potential discomfort.

When you embrace vulnerability in your relationships, you create opportunities for growth, healing, and mutual understanding. You allow yourself to be fully seen and known by others, and in doing so, you cultivate a sense of belonging and acceptance that is essential for building strong, resilient connections.

So, dare to be vulnerable in your relationships. Embrace your imperfections, share your fears and insecurities, and allow yourself to be fully present with others. In doing so, you'll discover the transformative power of vulnerability in fostering courageous relationships built on trust, authenticity, and mutual respect.

Fostering Trust in Courageous Relationships

Trust is the foundation of any meaningful relationship, and in courageous relationships, it takes on an even deeper significance. Trust is the confidence and reliability you have in someone or something, knowing that they will act with integrity and have your best interests at heart.

In courageous relationships, trust is not simply built on promises or words alone but on consistent actions and behaviors that demonstrate reliability, honesty, and respect. It's about showing up for each other, being dependable, and following through on commitments.

Trust is earned over time through shared experiences, mutual respect, and effective communication. When you trust someone, you feel safe and secure in their presence, knowing they will support you, listen to you, and honor your feelings and boundaries.

Building trust in relationships requires vulnerability and courage. It means being willing to let down your guard, be open and honest, and take risks, even when there's a chance of getting hurt. It's about showing empathy and understanding, being transparent and accountable, and demonstrating your commitment to the relationship through your actions.

In courageous relationships, trust is not assumed but actively cultivated and nurtured. It requires ongoing effort and communication to maintain, as well as forgiveness and grace when mistakes are made. Trust is fragile and can be easily broken, but when it's present, it forms the foundation for deep, meaningful connections that can withstand the tests of time and adversity.

So, nurture trust in your relationships. Be consistent, reliable, and honest. Show up for each other, listen with empathy, and communicate openly and authentically. By fostering trust in your relationships, you'll create a safe and supportive environment where you can truly be yourself and experience the transformative power of courageous connections.

As this chapter on courageous relationships draws to a close, remember that communication, vulnerability, and trust are the keys to fostering deeper connections and creating environments of mutual respect and understanding. If you embrace these elements in your personal and professional relationships, you can cultivate the courage to navigate challenges together and form bonds that withstand the tests of time.

Now you know how to strengthen relationships, let's shift the focus to you. In the next chapter, we'll move on to the topic of self-doubt and how it can impact our ability to lead courageously.

I hope you're ready to explore strategies for overcoming self-doubt and embrace your full potential as a courageous leader.

References

50 Powerful Leadership Quotes to Inspire Your Organization (2023, February 22). Qualtrics.

https://www.qualtrics.com/blog/50-powerful-leadership-quotes/

Barnes, S. (2021, December 20). *How Vulnerability Makes You More Courageous and Improves Your Relationships.*

https://motivatedprogress.com/vulnerability/?utm_content=cmp-true

Chambers, A M. (2023, July 26). *How to Improve Your Relationships – Both Personally and Professionally.* Entrepreneur.

https://www.entrepreneur.com/growing-a-business/how-to-improve-your-relationships-both-personally-and/454062

Chidgey, H. (2024, February 21). The Essence of Leadership: Courage, Integrity, and Relationships.

https://www.linkedin.com/pulse/essence-leadership-courage-integrity-relationships-henry-chidgey-wzyzc/

Cory, D. (2024, April 5). Courage, Leadership, and your Emotional Intelligence.

https://www.linkedin.com/pulse/courage-leadership-your-emotional-intelligence-david-cory-ma-pcc-qhdnc/

Courage to Connect: Why Great Leaders Build Deep Bonds in Difficult Times. (2021, March 12) Rohei.com

https://www.rohei.com/resources/courage-to-connect-why-great-leaders-build-deep-bonds-in-difficult-times

Eisler, M. (2023, October 19). *Courageous Communication.* Wide Lens.

https://widelensleadership.com/courageous-communication/

Leading Authentically Through Vulnerability. Leadership Inspiration.

https://leadershipinspirations.com/leading-authentically-through-vulnerability/

May, B. (2023, July 6). *Vulnerability: The True Strength of Leadership.*

https://www.linkedin.com/pulse/vulnerability-true-strength-leadership-ben-may/

Relationships and Communication. (2022, February 24). Better Health.

https://www.betterhealth.vic.gov.au/health/healthyliving/relationships-and-communication

Schrader, J. (2015, October 7). *Courage in Relationships: Conquering Vulnerability and Fear.* Psychology Today.

https://www.psychologytoday.com/us/blog/evolution-the-self/201510/courage-in-relationships-conquering-vulnerability-and-fear

Schwartz, A. (2013, August 2). *Relationships and the Meaning of Courage.*

https://www.mentalhelp.net/blogs/relationships-and-the-meaning-of-courage/

Seltzer, LF. (2015, October 7). *Courage in Relationships: Conquering Vulnerability and Fear.* Psychology Today.

https://www.psychologytoday.com/gb/blog/evolution-the-self/201510/courage-in-relationships-conquering-vulnerability-and-fear

Winston, D. (2024, June 21). *How to Navigate Shifting Power Dynamics in Relationships, According to Experts.*

https://www.success.com/ways-to-navigate-power-dynamics-in-relationships/

Zenger, J. Folkman, J. (2019, February 5). *The 3 Elements of Trust.* Harvard Business Review.

https://hbr.org/2019/02/the-3-elements-of-trust

Chapter 7

Overcoming Self-Doubt

Self-doubt is debilitating. It's something that can creep up on you and dim the light of your courageousness. In your journey toward courageous leadership, there inevitably comes a point where you find yourself facing your own doubts and insecurities. Trust me, this is a normal process. You see, self-doubt has a way of casting shadows over our abilities and clouding our judgment. It's a formidable opponent, one that can paralyze us with fear and keep us from reaching our full potential.

I'm here to tell you that you don't have to let that happen!

In comparison, your self-belief is a powerful tool that can help you grow and develop. It shines best when it's not overshadowed by self-doubt, and it's something you can tap into to keep yourself motivated. It's all about using that belief to learn and move forward.

Roosevelt gets it right here:

"Believe you can and you're halfway there." ~ Theodore Roosevelt

In this chapter, we'll confront the adversary of self-doubt head-on and work on building your self-belief. You'll explore what self-doubt is and how it can impact you and others, shedding light on the internal struggles that often hinder courageous actions. From the fear of failure to the nagging voice of impostor syndrome, we'll consider the various ways self-doubt manifests and holds us back. You may be surprised to see how common self-doubt is!

Don't worry; we'll also be arming ourselves with practical strategies for building your self-confidence and self-belief. This chapter will share actionable steps you can take to silence the inner critic and cultivate a mindset of resilience and empowerment. By embracing your strengths, acknowledging your achievements, and challenging your limiting beliefs, you can begin to pave the way toward greater self-assurance.

Ultimately, we'll come to understand the intimate connection between confidence and courageous fire. As leaders, our ability to inspire and motivate others is deeply rooted in our sense of self-assurance. By nurturing our confidence, we not only embolden ourselves to take bold action but also empower those around us to do the same.

It's time to clarify what self-doubt is and talk more about overcoming it so you can become more courageous than ever before.

What Is Self-Doubt and How Can It Impact Me?

I know you've heard it. That nagging voice of uncertainty and fear we call self-doubt. It can wield significant power over our thoughts, emotions, and actions. It's the whisper that tells us we're not good enough, smart enough, or even capable enough to succeed. Self-doubt can manifest in various forms, from questioning our own abilities and second-guessing our decisions to comparing ourselves unfavorably to others. If we don't stop it in its tracks, it tightens its grip, and it can become more difficult to break free. Nevertheless, breaking free is still possible, and later, we'll talk through some strategies to help you do just that.

You're probably wondering why self-doubt is a major focus, and that's because the impact of self-doubt can be profound, influencing every aspect of our lives. It can undermine our confidence, erode our self-esteem, and hinder our progress toward our goals. When we doubt ourselves, it's not uncommon for us to hesitate when taking risks or pursuing opportunities, fearing failure or rejection. This hesitation can lead to missed opportunities, stagnant growth, and a pervasive sense of dissatisfaction with our lives.

Self-doubt can also take a toll on our mental and emotional well-being, contributing to feelings of anxiety, stress, and depression. It can rob us of our peace of mind, leaving us trapped in a cycle of negative thinking and self-criticism. Over time, chronic self-doubt can chip away at our resilience and optimism, leaving us feeling defeated and disillusioned. By now, I'm sure you're beginning to understand how it can impact your courageous fire—*how can we be courageous with self-doubt lurking?*

In the realm of leadership, self-doubt can be particularly insidious, as it can undermine our ability to inspire and motivate others. Leaders who are plagued by self-doubt may struggle to make confident decisions, communicate effectively, or assert their authority. This can create a ripple effect throughout an organization, impacting morale, productivity, and overall performance.

To put this into perspective, consider this: You want to hire someone to fix something at home, and it's going to cost a lot of money. One potential contractor who looks at the job says, "I think I'll be able to fix *this*," but doesn't sound sure. They're supposed to be qualified, experienced, and capable, but they don't sound confident they can help. Another contractor comes along and explains how they can do the job, how long it can take, how much it will cost (and maybe it's a little more expensive), and they confirm that they can definitely do this with ease, confidently. *Who do you put your faith in and trust to do this job?*

Of course, you're going to choose the person who is confident and doesn't doubt themselves. Their belief in themselves makes you believe them, too. And when it comes to leadership, it's the same concept. A confident leader who isn't plagued with self-doubt will instill confidence in their team members.

Self-doubt is like a dark cloud that looms overhead, casting a shadow over our potential and obscuring our path forward. Yet, by shining a light on our doubts and acknowledging their presence, we can begin to take steps toward overcoming them. Through self-awareness, self-compassion, and intentional action, we can challenge our limiting beliefs and reclaim our confidence.

How Can Self-Doubt Hinder Courage?

It's difficult to be courageous if you doubt yourself. Self-doubt can be like a persistent shadow. It casts doubt on our abilities, clouds our judgment, and stifles our courage. It acts as an internal barrier, obstructing the path to bold action and keeping us firmly stuck in our comfort zone. When plagued by self-doubt, even the most promising opportunities can appear daunting, and the fear of failure looms, paralyzing us from taking the necessary steps toward our goals.

But you don't have to let it!

Self-doubt is capable of extinguishing the flames of your courageous fire. It often manifests as negative self-talk, undermining your confidence first before reinforcing limiting beliefs about your capabilities. It whispers doubts about your worthiness, competence, and potential for success, eroding your self-esteem and fueling feelings of inadequacy. As a result, your courage is impacted, and you may hesitate to seize opportunities, second-guess your decisions, and shy away from challenges that could lead to growth and fulfillment.

Self-doubt serves no one!

Moreover, self-doubt can create a self-perpetuating cycle of inaction, as our fear of failure reinforces our doubts and also makes us reluctant to take risks. I've been there. I've felt the doubt and lived the stagnation it causes, so that's why I know self-doubt doesn't serve you. It's a hindrance. Instead of embracing uncertainty and viewing setbacks as opportunities for learning and growth, we retreat into the safety of familiarity, clinging to the status quo rather than venturing into the unknown. *You already know how I feel about the status quo!*

Self-doubt can undermine your ability to inspire and motivate others when you're a leader, as your own insecurities may project onto those you lead. It can diminish your credibility as a leader and weaken the bonds of trust and respect within your team. When leaders succumb to self-doubt, they may hesitate to make difficult decisions, shy away from challenging conversations, and avoid taking responsibility for their actions—all of which can destroy morale and impede organizational progress.

Ultimately, self-doubt robs us of the opportunity to realize our full potential and live authentically. It confines us to a narrow existence governed by fear and uncertainty, preventing us from embracing our inherent worthiness and embracing the courage required to pursue our dreams. However, by recognizing how self-doubt operates and actively challenging our limiting beliefs, we can reclaim our power, cultivate resilience, and chart a course toward a more courageous and fulfilling life.

Reflection Time

Take some time to assess your self-doubt by reflecting on your own experiences. Think about how they have impacted your life, and consider the questions below:

- How does self-doubt manifest in your thoughts and behaviors?

- Are there recurring patterns or triggers that exacerbate your feelings of doubt and insecurity?

Reflect on a recent situation where self-doubt prevented you from taking a courageous action or pursuing a goal.

- What were the thoughts or beliefs that held you back?

- How did you feel at that moment?

Think about how self-doubt has influenced your decision-making process.

- Have you ever second-guessed yourself or hesitated to speak up due to fear of failure or rejection?

Consider the long-term effects of self-doubt on your personal and professional development.

- How has it impacted your confidence, self-esteem, and overall well-being?

- In what ways has it hindered your growth and success?

Imagine a scenario in which you are able to overcome self-doubt and take courageous action.

- What would that look like?

- How would it feel to step outside your comfort zone and embrace the unknown?

Be honest with yourself as you reflect on these questions and acknowledge how self-doubt may be holding you back.

Remember that self-awareness is the first step toward personal growth and empowerment. If you confront your doubts and challenge your limiting beliefs, you can cultivate the courage and resilience needed to pursue your aspirations and live authentically.

How I Used My Courageous Fire to Overcome Self-Doubt

There are several times in my life when I've had doubts about myself. I've contemplated my abilities and doubted what I was doing several times, what I should be doing or not doing. One story in particular that I'm drawn to tell you pertains to courageous fire and is very relevant to this chapter.

Following the pandemic's upheaval, I found myself navigating a time of doubt and uncertainty. Amidst the chaos, my professional journey took an unexpected turn as I transitioned from the role of superintendent to assistant superintendent of human resources, a role I have previously served in. Almost two years later, in 2022, as the world gradually emerged from the grips of COVID-19, I returned to superintendency. I then attended my first national conference since 2019, surrounded by fellow educators and leaders. Yet, despite being among esteemed colleagues and thought leaders, I couldn't shake the nagging feeling of inadequacy.

Was I meant to even be here?

Sitting in the audience, listening to the presenters, I couldn't help but feel out of place. Questions swirled in my mind, each one amplifying the sense of self-doubt that had taken root within me. *What was I doing or not doing? Why did I feel so behind? What was I missing?* The weight of these doubts pressed upon me, urging me to question my abilities and worth. *Where had my confidence gone?*

Despite feeling so out of the loop with current information and the lingering turmoil of self-doubt, I knew something had to change. A flicker of determination emerged, and I realized that I had the power to change my narrative. I wasn't exactly the type of person who would give up easily. So, I set some goals and set my sights firmly on achieving them. One goal was to become a part of the national advisory board for the organization hosting the conference. This was an ambitious goal but one

I pursued with unwavering determination. Another goal was to become a keynote speaker at one of their conferences.

With each passing day, I poured my energy into honing my skills and expanding my knowledge. I immersed myself in my work, seizing every opportunity to learn and grow. Fast-forward a year later, to the end of 2022, I was accepted as a board member and asked to keynote at one of their speaker events. These achievements are a testament to the power of perseverance and self-belief. I've recently been asked to keynote again at a larger conference event.

Reflecting on this journey made me realize that self-doubt is a natural part of the human experience. I share this story because I know what it's like to feel like I am not good enough (in my own head). It's easy to succumb to feelings of inadequacy and insecurity, especially in the face of uncertainty. But beneath the surface of doubt lies an untapped reservoir of strength and resilience. It's only when we challenge our doubts and push past our limitations that we discover the boundless potential within us. You have this in you, too.

So, to anyone grappling with self-doubt, I offer this advice: Embrace your doubts but don't let them define you. Instead, let them serve as a catalyst for growth and transformation. Believe in your abilities, trust in your journey, and never lose sight of the courageous fire burning within you. Those flames of self-doubt are what we use to forge the steel of our tenacity so that we can emerge stronger, wiser, and more resilient and confident than ever before.

How to Build Your Confidence and Belief in Yourself

If your confidence and self-belief are something you struggle with, it's time to take immediate action. There are some practical steps you can take to help cultivate both confidence and belief in yourself.

Let's take a look at some of those:

1. Set Realistic Goals

    I mentioned in my personal story that I set some goals, and I can't recommend it enough. Break down your larger goals into smaller, more manageable tasks. Celebrate your achievements along the way, no matter how small they may seem. Each step forward will reinforce your belief in your abilities.

2. Challenge Negative Self-Talk

    Pay attention to your inner dialogue and challenge negative thoughts or beliefs about yourself. Replace self-critical statements with affirmations and positive affirmations that reinforce your worth and capabilities.

3. Practice Self-Compassion

    Treat yourself with kindness and understanding, especially when facing setbacks or challenges. Embrace failure as an opportunity for growth and learning rather than a reflection of your worth.

4. Step Out of Your Comfort Zone

    Take calculated risks and push yourself outside of your comfort zone. Embrace new experiences and challenges as opportunities to expand your skills and build confidence in your ability to adapt and succeed.

5. Surround Yourself with Supportive People

    Surround yourself with people who believe in you and support your goals. Seek out mentors, coaches, or friends who can provide encouragement, guidance, and perspective during times of doubt.

6. Focus on Your Strengths

    Identify your strengths and unique talents and leverage them to achieve your goals. Celebrate your achievements and recognize your value as an individual with unique strengths and contributions to offer.

7. Practice Self-Care

    Prioritize self-care activities that nourish your mind, body, and spirit. Engage in activities that bring you joy, relaxation, and fulfillment, and prioritize your physical and emotional well-being.

8. Visualize Success

    Use visualization techniques to imagine yourself achieving your goals and overcoming obstacles. Visualizing success can help build confidence and reinforce your belief in your ability to achieve your aspirations.

If you incorporate these strategies into your daily life, you can gradually build confidence and self-belief, enabling you to pursue your goals with courage, resilience, and determination. Working on yourself improves your ability to lead with confidence and instill that confidence and self-belief within your team members.

Remember, change doesn't happen overnight. Building confidence is a process that takes time, so be patient and compassionate with yourself along the way.

Confidence and Courageous Fire

This book is all about courageous leadership, and confidence is a vital ingredient of this. When you possess confidence in yourself and your abilities, you radiate an aura of authority and assurance that inspires trust and respect in those around you. You can feel it, and others can see it from a mile away. It's time to focus on the links between confidence and your courageous fire as you lead others.

There's no doubt that confidence breeds trust between you and your team. When you believe in yourself and your vision, others are more likely to trust your judgment and follow your lead. Your confidence offers a sense of assurance and stability, encouraging others to rally behind you in pursuit of common goals. Together, your confidence and courage help you to motivate your team consistently.

Courageous leadership often involves taking calculated risks and stepping into the unknown. When you have confidence in your decision-making abilities and capacity to handle challenges, you're more willing to venture outside your comfort zone and explore new opportunities for growth and innovation. Even if things don't always work out, that confidence fuels your courage and encourages you to try something new. That courageousness you feel also allows you to acknowledge when something hasn't worked out so you can learn, problem-solve, and move forward.

True confidence allows you to embrace vulnerability and authenticity in your leadership style. This, too, is a courageous action because showing your vulnerable side can be a difficult thing. If you're comfortable showing your human side, acknowledging your strengths and weaknesses, and being open to feedback and collaboration, you're showing courage to the rest of your team. Your willingness to be vulnerable fosters deeper connections with your team members and cultivates a culture of trust and transparency.

Confidence is a powerful shield against adversity, and while we've talked about adversity already, this is a really important link between confidence and courageous leadership. When faced with obstacles or setbacks, confident leaders maintain their composure and resilience, viewing challenges as opportunities for growth rather than insurmountable barriers.

Their unwavering self-assurance enables them to persevere in the face of adversity, inspiring others to do the same.

I've been lucky enough to have been mentored by many confident leaders throughout my working life who have been (and still are) positive role models. I appreciate the positive impact that confident and courageous leaders have on others. Confident leaders empower others to realize their full potential and contribute their unique talents to the collective effort. By demonstrating confidence in their team members' abilities and providing them with autonomy and support, they create an environment where individuals feel empowered to take the initiative, express their ideas, and pursue excellence.

Confidence is certainly an essential attribute of courageous leadership. As you cultivate confidence within yourself, you'll find that your courageous fire burns brighter, illuminating the path forward and inspiring others to join you on the journey toward shared success.

It's essential to reflect on the transformative journey of overcoming self-doubt as we bring this chapter to a close. Throughout this chapter, we've explored the depths of self-doubt, uncovering its pervasive influence on our actions and decisions while examining how self-doubt can hinder courageous actions, keeping us trapped in a cycle of uncertainty and fear.

Yet, in recognizing the power of self-awareness and self-belief, we've discovered that self-doubt need not define our destiny. If you acknowledge your internal struggles and begin to understand the impact, you've taken the first steps toward liberation and empowerment. You've explored practical strategies for building confidence and self-belief, equipping yourself with the tools needed to confront self-doubt head-on and emerge victorious.

Self-doubt is something we need to keep in check, so as we move on, let's embrace the next chapter as we focus on forgiveness. Next, we'll dive into the profound act of forgiveness and its transformative potential in our lives. Just as we've confronted our internal doubts and fears, we should confront the resentment and bitterness and head on our path of healing and reconciliation.

References

Ackerman, C E. (2018, July 18). *Building Strong Self-Belief: 16 Tips and Activities.* Positivepsychology.com

https://positivepsychology.com/self-confidence-self-belief/

Davis, T. (2023, December 12). *How to Overcome Self-Doubt.* Psychology Today.

https://www.psychologytoday.com/intl/blog/click-here-happiness/202205/how-overcome-self-doubt

Developing Self-Confidence as a Leader. (2023, December 20).

https://management30.com/blog/self-confidence/

How to Build Self-Confidence. Mindtools.

https://www.mindtools.com/ap5omwt/how-to-build-self-confidence

Morin, A. (2024, April 25). *How to Be More Confident: 9 Tips That Work.* Verywellmind.

https://www.verywellmind.com/how-to-boost-your-self-confidence-4163098

Saxena, S. (2022, May 2). *Self-Doubt: What it is, Signs, & How to Overcome.* Choosing Therapy.

https://www.choosingtherapy.com/self-doubt/#:~:text=Having%20severe%20issues%20with%20self,you%20have%20self%2Ddoubt%20include%3A&text=Feeling%20worthless,Having%20a%20loud%20inner%20critic

Warrell, M. (2017, December 9). *How to Beat Self-Doubt and Stop Selling Yourself Short.* Forbes.

https://www.forbes.com/sites/margiewarrell/2017/12/09/doubt-your-doubts/

Williams, JM. (2023, April 18). *Conquer Your Inner Critic: Overcoming Self-Doubt and Unleashing Your Potential - #2*

https://www.linkedin.com/pulse/conquer-your-inner-critic-overcoming-self-doubt-2-williams-ed-d/

Yuen-Ting Chui, A. *How Self-Doubt Keeps You Stuck (And How to Overcome It)*. LifeHack.

https://www.lifehack.org/567587/the-reasons-of-self-doubt-and-steps-to-deal-`with-it

Chapter 8

The Courage to Forgive

Forgiveness can be a complicated concept. Simply saying you forgive doesn't mean you can expect this just to happen. You've got to mean it, and you've got to feel that forgiveness too. It wasn't until I came to realize that it takes courage to truly forgive someone, however, it's good for the soul—as Willis says:

> *"Holding a grudge doesn't make you strong; it makes you bitter. Forgiving doesn't make you weak; it sets you free."* ~ Dave Willis

You see, forgiveness is also an act of courage that holds transformative power. In this chapter, we'll explore the depth of forgiveness, its healing capabilities, and the strength it requires because forgiveness is not an easy thing. As leaders, the ability to forgive is not only essential for personal growth but also for fostering healthy relationships and creating a positive organizational culture. *This is ultimately what we want, right?*

Throughout history, forgiveness has been recognized as a key component of resilience and compassion. It allows us to release the burdens of the past and embrace the present with clarity and grace. But as already mentioned, forgiveness is difficult; it demands vulnerability, humility, and a willingness to let go of resentment and anger.

We need to start understanding forgiveness at a deeper level, so we'll dive into its transformative effects on both people and communities. We'll begin to examine how a simple act of forgiveness breaks the cycle of pain and suffering, leading to healing and reconciliation. We'll also take some time to discuss the importance of forgiveness in personal development, highlighting its role in letting go of past grievances and embracing a future filled with possibility.

There's no doubt that forgiveness is a courageous act, so let us discover the profound impact it can have on our lives and leadership journey.

What Does It Mean to Forgive?

Forgiveness is a complex and deeply personal concept, often intertwined with emotions of hurt, anger, and resentment. At its core, forgiveness involves a conscious decision to let go of negative feelings and release the desire for revenge or retaliation against those who have wronged us.

I just want to clarify that forgiveness doesn't mean condoning or excusing the hurtful actions of others. Instead, it signifies a willingness to move forward without carrying the burden of past grievances. It's a conscious choice to free ourselves from the emotional weight of resentment, which can weigh heavy on us. It can consume our thoughts and hinder our personal growth—this has no benefit to us or anyone else. When I realized this, I started to think differently about forgiveness.

When we forgive, we let go of the power our past holds over us. We choose to break free from the cycle of pain and negativity, allowing ourselves to experience inner peace and emotional healing. Forgiveness is an act of self-compassion, as it permits us to prioritize our well-being over feelings of bitterness or resentment.

Forgiveness isn't solely for the benefit of the person being forgiven; it's also a gift we give to ourselves. If we let go of grudges and embrace forgiveness, it creates space for love, compassion, and understanding. We open ourselves up to the possibility of reconciliation and renewed relationships, both with others and with ourselves.

Embracing forgiveness is an act of courage and strength. It requires vulnerability and humility to confront past hurts and choose the path of forgiveness. As leaders, cultivating a culture of forgiveness within us and our organizations can foster greater resilience, empathy, and unity.

The Healing Power of Forgiveness

There's something very healing about forgiveness. It's not merely an act of letting go and moving on; it's a deeply transformative process that liberates us from resentment's shackles, anger, and bitterness. It takes a lot of inner strength. When we forgive, we embrace self-discovery and emotional liberation, paving the way for profound healing and inner peace.

Forgiveness makes us feel better. It holds the remarkable ability to mend the wounds of the past and restore harmony within ourselves and our relationships. By releasing the grip of past hurts and grievances, we create space for healing to happen, allowing for the emergence of joy, compassion, and renewed vitality. Holding a grudge isn't a nice feeling, but through forgiveness, we free ourselves of that feeling.

Forgiveness heals by restoring our sense of wholeness and well-being. For ourselves, we don't need to hold onto the negative stuff. When we do, we create a barrier that prevents us from fully experiencing life's beauty and abundance. Forgiveness dismantles this barrier, allowing us to reconnect with our innate sense of worthiness and belonging. Letting go of the past allows us to open ourselves up to greater levels of self-acceptance and self-compassion, nurturing a deeper sense of inner peace and contentment.

We don't always acknowledge the strength of forgiveness, as it has the power to help us mend fractured relationships and cultivate deeper connections with others. When we forgive, we create opportunities for reconciliation and healing, fostering greater empathy, understanding, and compassion in our interactions. Embracing forgiveness means we're breaking down the walls of separation and division and paving the way for both authentic connection and mutual respect.

We haven't even covered the mental, emotional, and physical well-being benefits of forgiveness, but research has shown that practicing forgiveness can lead to reduced levels of stress, anxiety, and depression, as well as improved overall health and longevity. By releasing the grip of resentment and anger, we free ourselves from the toxic effects of chronic negativity, allowing for greater emotional resilience and vitality.

Forgiveness and Its Transformative Effects

The best way to gain a stronger understanding of forgiveness and its transformative effects is to explore some real-life stories. Through powerful stories of resilience and reconciliation, you can see how forgiveness has the remarkable ability to heal wounds, transcend hatred, and pave the way for profound personal and societal transformation.

- *Nelson Mandela*

  After spending twenty-seven years in prison during South Africa's apartheid era, Mandela forgave his captors and oppressors upon his release. Instead of seeking revenge, he advocated for reconciliation and forgiveness, leading South Africa toward a peaceful transition to democracy. His forgiveness transformed the nation, inspiring people around the world to pursue forgiveness and reconciliation in the face of injustice.

- *Anne Frank's Father*

  Otto Frank, the father of Anne Frank, forgave the Nazi officer who betrayed his family to the authorities during World War II. Despite enduring unimaginable suffering and loss, Otto chose to forgive, demonstrating the transformative power of forgiveness in overcoming hatred and fostering reconciliation.

- *Immaculée Ilibagiza*

  Immaculée, a survivor of the Rwandan genocide, forgave the perpetrators who killed her family during the ethnic violence. Through forgiveness, she was able to transcend the trauma of her past and rebuild her life with a sense of peace and purpose. Immaculée's story exemplifies the transformative effects of forgiveness in overcoming hatred and fostering healing.

- *Pope John Paul II and Mehmet Ali Agca*

  In 1983, Mehmet Ali Agca attempted to assassinate Pope John Paul II in St. Peter's Square. Despite being shot and gravely wounded, the Pope forgave Agca and even visited him in prison to offer his forgiveness in person. This act of forgiveness not only transformed Agca's life but also inspired countless others to embrace forgiveness as a path to reconciliation and healing.

- *Desmond Tutu*

  As a prominent figure in South Africa's anti-apartheid movement, Archbishop Desmond Tutu played a crucial role in promoting forgiveness and reconciliation in the post-apartheid era. Through his leadership of the Truth and Reconciliation Commission, Tutu helped facilitate dialogue and forgiveness between victims and perpetrators of apartheid-era crimes, fostering healing and reconciliation across the nation.

These stories highlight the transformative effects of forgiveness, demonstrating how it can transcend hatred, heal wounds, and pave the way for reconciliation and peace. There's no doubt that it takes courage to forgive, and when we do, we set a positive example to others.

Where would we be without forgiveness?

Reflection Time

Reflect on a time when you've experienced hurt or disappointment, and consider whether you've been able to forgive.

- If so, how do you think forgiveness contributed toward your healing and growth?

- If not, what barriers prevented you from forgiving, and what steps could you take toward forgiveness for your own well-being?

A Story of Forgiveness

Forgiveness is a difficult chapter for me because there are some things I'm still working on personally. Forgiveness doesn't always come easy. Don't get me wrong, there are moments in my life that I've been able to forgive, and I recognize those who have had a significant impact on me. But as I write, I realize I'm still navigating the forgiveness journey regarding a few other issues in my life. This is challenging at times. Forgiveness can be tough, but I know firsthand that it's important.

In my professional life, I encountered a situation where I had a supervisor who struggled with competence. They were hired based on a previous professional relationship with the "big boss," but when they came into the role, they lacked the necessary technical skills and were unwilling to learn those all-important technical components of the job. This put a huge strain on the workforce and workspace I was working in at the time.

I was left with the responsibility of continuing to lead the work in the department and moving tasks forward, as this was extremely challenging for my supervisor. Over time, the staff in that department and throughout the organization started coming to me for answers, guidance, and support. I really believe that my supervisor sensed this shift and realized they were not being approached as the ultimate authority like they should have been. This took its toll on everyone.

Relationships between the supervisor and staff were strained, and eventually, the supervisor resigned due to their inability to fulfill the job responsibilities. During this period, other departments needed information and support, too. Times were tough. The organization was going through a massive organizational restructuring process at the time—a legal, emotional, and impactful procedure involving an administrative law judge and attorneys. I was often asked to provide answers behind the scenes when my supervisor couldn't navigate the changes. This was an awful time, especially for those potentially impacted, and tensions were high.

One day, an executive in another department became very frustrated because the situation was affecting site administrators, teachers, and staff throughout the organization. This person yelled and screamed at me, and although this may sound exaggerated, I felt attacked. I felt I was being treated unfairly and held responsible for something I couldn't control. This wasn't my doing, and I took it personally. I lashed back. The executive continued to criticize me, emphasizing the impact and lack of decision-making. I didn't know what to do or where to turn.

It's rare for me to feel at a loss for how to respond to an attack on my work and move forward, but that day, I did. I left work that day, something I'd never done before, and went home feeling demoralized. While I don't think the person intended to make me feel this way, that was the result. I believe I cried on the way home after the incident—not in the moment, but later. I was so frustrated.

I'm a professional, so I moved on, composed myself, and continued my work. But I didn't forget that experience.

As time went on, my path directly crossed with this executive in several professional settings. Although there was some distance between us, I realized I hadn't fully moved past this event. I needed to forgive and let go of that resentment.

Recently, I attended a professional learning event. There was an activity about letting go of burdens, and in the activity, we had to describe something that we needed to let go of in order to potentially grow. As I looked around the room, I realized that I was in the same space as this executive, and I knew in that moment that I had fully let go of the experience that had once demoralized me.

In the true sense of having forgiveness come full circle, I have since had the opportunity to support this individual with some challenges that have been impactful in their life.

Forgiveness is possible and one thing I've come to realize is that forgiveness is freeing, but it takes time and courage to be able to truly move on. I still have a few situations where I'm on the journey to forgiveness (I'm not quite there yet), but once I do, I'll be free and clear of those lingering thoughts and emotions.

Forgiveness isn't easy, but it's a powerful step toward healing and growth.

Finding the Courage to Forgive

Now, I keep telling you that forgiveness takes courage, but I haven't really provided you with any practical guidance on this yet. Don't worry; practical advice is on the way to you in this section.

Finding the courage to forgive is a deeply personal and often challenging journey. It requires us to confront our pain, let go of resentment, and open ourselves to vulnerability. Yet, despite its difficulty, forgiveness is a powerful act of courage that can liberate us from the shackles of anger and bitterness, allowing us to move forward with grace and peace.

Here are some practical strategies to help you find the courage to forgive:

- Acknowledge your pain – Yes, it hurts sometimes, but before you can begin the process of forgiveness, it's essential to acknowledge the pain that you've experienced. Allow yourself to feel the full range of emotions that accompany hurt and betrayal. By acknowledging your pain, you validate your feelings and lay the groundwork for healing.

- Understand the benefits of forgiveness – Forgiveness is not about excusing or condoning the actions of others; it's about freeing yourself from the burden of resentment. Recognize that holding onto anger only prolongs your suffering, while forgiveness offers the possibility of inner peace and emotional freedom.

- Cultivate empathy – Try to see the situation from the perspective of the person who wronged you. Recognize that everyone makes mistakes and that hurtful actions are often the result of pain or ignorance. Cultivating empathy can soften your heart and make forgiveness feel more attainable.

- Practice self-compassion – Just as you would extend compassion to a friend who is struggling, offer yourself the same kindness and understanding. Acknowledge that forgiveness is a process and that it's okay to feel hesitant or resistant. Treat yourself with patience and gentleness as you navigate this journey.

- Set boundaries – Forgiveness does not mean condoning harmful behavior or allowing yourself to be mistreated. It's essential to set boundaries to protect yourself from further harm while still extending compassion to the person who hurt you. Clearly communicate your boundaries and be prepared to enforce them if necessary.

- Release resentment – Holding onto resentment only poisons your own heart and mind. Practice letting go of resentment by journaling, meditating, or engaging in other self-care activities. Release the grip of negative emotions and make space for healing and growth.

- Seek support – Forgiveness can be a challenging process, and it's okay to ask for help along the way. Reach out to trusted friends, family members, or a therapist who can offer guidance, support, and perspective. Sharing your feelings with others can help you feel less alone and more empowered on your journey toward forgiveness.

- Practice gratitude – Cultivate a sense of gratitude for the lessons you've learned and the strength you've gained from your experiences. Focus on the positive aspects of your life and the people who support and love you unconditionally. Gratitude can shift your perspective and help you find peace amidst pain.

- Choose forgiveness – Only you can do this! Ultimately, forgiveness is a choice that you must make for yourself. It's not about forgetting or condoning the past but about reclaiming your power and embracing the possibility of a brighter future. Choose forgiveness as an act of courage and self-love, knowing that it has the power to set you free.

Finding the courage to forgive isn't easy, but it's worth the effort. By embracing forgiveness, you can release yourself from the chains of the past and step into a future filled with compassion and possibility.

Allow yourself to be brave, to dig deep, and to choose the path of forgiveness. In doing so, you'll discover the transformative power of courage and healing that comes from letting go.

In leadership, the ability to forgive is an invaluable skill that fosters trust, promotes collaboration, and strengthens relationships within teams and organizations. If you apply these techniques to leadership roles, you can create a culture of accountability, empathy, and resilience. When leaders demonstrate the courage to forgive, they model vulnerability and authenticity, inspiring others to do the same.

Leaders who prioritize forgiveness cultivate environments where others feel safe to take risks, learn from mistakes, and grow personally and professionally. This sets the scene for others to follow. If you integrate forgiveness into your leadership approach, you will not only enhance your own well-being but also empower those around you to thrive in an atmosphere of compassion while still displaying courage.

Personal Development: Learning to Forgive and What That Means

As leaders, professional development is just as important as personal development. They are not a luxury but a necessity, as learning and growing are a must! I've also found that personal development has a positive impact on us professionally and vice versa. That's because any kind of learning and development = growth. Your own personal development can help you form your own leadership style.

It's time to explore the importance of personal leadership growth and how it directly impacts our ability to lead effectively. We'll talk through various strategies, including forgiveness in the workplace, problem-solving techniques, and other tools for personal development. Through these experiences, we'll uncover how forgiveness can be a powerful catalyst for growth, both personally and professionally.

Forgiveness in the Workplace

Forgiveness is often seen as a personal virtue, but its application in the workplace can have positive effects on organizational culture and team dynamics. Leaders who cultivate a culture of forgiveness foster an environment where employees feel valued, respected, and supported. This can lead to improved collaboration, productivity, and overall job satisfaction. Strategies for integrating forgiveness into the workplace may include fostering open communication, providing opportunities for reconciliation, and promoting empathy and understanding among team members.

Problem-solving and Personal Growth

Facing challenges and overcoming obstacles are inherent parts of leadership. When approached with a mindset of forgiveness, these experiences can become opportunities for personal growth and development. By reframing setbacks as learning opportunities and practicing forgiveness toward ourselves and others, we can cultivate resilience, adaptability, and emotional intelligence. Problem-solving techniques such as active listening, seeking feedback, and embracing creativity can further enhance our ability to navigate difficult situations and foster positive outcomes.

The Developmental Impact of Forgiveness

Forgiveness is not just about letting go of past grievances; it's about freeing ourselves from the burden of resentment and opening ourselves up to new possibilities. As leaders, learning to forgive allows us to cultivate greater self-awareness, emotional maturity, and relational intelligence. By practicing forgiveness in our professional lives, we not only foster healthier work environments but also pave the way for personal growth and development. Through forgiveness, we can deepen our understanding of ourselves and others, build stronger connections, and ultimately become more effective and compassionate leaders.

Better Mental Health and Well-Being

Research shows that holding onto grudges and resentment can have detrimental effects on mental health and overall well-being. When we refuse to forgive, we often experience heightened levels of stress, anxiety, and depression. These negative emotions can take a toll on our physical health, leading to an increased risk of conditions such as heart disease, high blood pressure, and compromised immune function.

That means forgiveness is good for your health!

Practicing forgiveness has been linked to improved mental health outcomes, including reduced symptoms of depression and anxiety, lower levels of stress, and greater overall life satisfaction. By releasing the grip of resentment and embracing forgiveness, we free ourselves from the emotional burden of past hurts so we can heal from those negative experiences.

In addition to its impact on mental health, forgiveness also plays a crucial role in promoting personal well-being. When we forgive others, we experience greater inner peace, contentment, and emotional resilience. Forgiveness, for many, fosters healthier relationships, both with others and with ourselves, as it encourages empathy, compassion, and understanding. By cultivating a mindset of forgiveness, we create a positive ripple effect in our lives, influencing our attitudes, behaviors, and overall sense of fulfillment.

Forgiveness is not just a passive act but a powerful tool for personal growth and development. When we choose to forgive, we demonstrate strength, resilience, and emotional maturity. Others will notice this and respect you. As a leader, respect is a crucial skill that will help you thrive.

When we learn to focus on the present moment, we free ourselves from the constraints of old wounds and limiting beliefs. Forgiveness enables us to cultivate greater self-awareness as we examine our own role in conflicts and relationships. It also fosters a sense of empathy and compassion as we take the perspectives and experiences of others into account. Ultimately, forgiveness empowers us to break free from cycles of negativity and move forward with clarity, purpose, and renewed vitality. As leaders, integrating forgiveness into our personal development journey can lead to greater effectiveness, authenticity, and impact in our professional roles and beyond.

As our exploration of forgiveness and its transformative power draws to a close, it's essential to recognize how it aligns with courageous fire in leadership. Just as forgiveness requires courage, resilience, and emotional strength, so too does effective leadership. If we embrace forgiveness, we heal old wounds and cultivate greater well-being while also demonstrating the courage to confront adversity and develop deeper connections with others.

This type of strength and courage is the foundation of a great leader!

In the context of leadership, the ability to forgive is a key component of courageous leadership, as it requires vulnerability, empathy, and a commitment to growth and transformation. Leaders who embody forgiveness create trust, collaboration, and innovation, which empowers their teams to thrive and achieve their full potential. If forgiveness is part of our leadership philosophy, we can inspire others to do the same, fostering cultures of compassion, resilience, and authenticity.

It's time for us to set the highest standards in leadership!

Remember, forgiveness is a transformative power that plays an integral role in cultivating courageous fire in leadership. In the next chapter, we'll shift our focus to the importance of cultivating courage in children and explore strategies to nurture resilience, empathy, and confidence in the next generation of leaders.

Are you ready to use that courage to empower young minds so they, too, can embrace courage, compassion, and possibility?

References

An Example of Finding Meaning in Deep Suffering: In Honor of Eva Mozes Kor. (2022, June 29). International Forgiveness.

https://internationalforgiveness.com/category/our-forgiveness-blog/courage/

Bank Lees, A. (2018, November 13). *Forgiveness: The Path to Healing and Emotional Freedom.* Psychology Today.

https://www.psychologytoday.com/us/blog/surviving-thriving/201811/forgiveness-the-path-healing-and-emotional-freedom

Brown, Harriet. *How to Forgive Anyone - and Why Your Health Depends on it.*

https://www.oprah.com/oprahs-lifeclass/how-to-forgive-others-health-benefits-of-forgiveness-fred-luskin/all

Colier, N. (2018, March 15). *What is Forgiveness and How Do You Do It?* Psychology Today.

https://www.psychologytoday.com/us/blog/inviting-monkey-tea/201803/what-is-forgiveness-and-how-do-you-do-it

Forbus, R. (2018, December 21) *Leaders and Forgiveness in the Workplace.*

https://www.linkedin.com/pulse/leaders-forgiveness-workplace-rick-forbus-phd/

Forgiveness: Letting go of grudges and bitterness. (2022, November 22) Mayo Clinic.

https://www.mayoclinic.org/healthy-lifestyle/adult-health/in-depth/forgiveness/art-20047692

How to Forgive Yourself and Others. (2024, April 4). Better Help.

https://www.betterhelp.com/advice/how-to/how-to-forgive-yourself-and-other/?utm_source=AdWords&utm_medium=Search_PPC_c&utm_term=PerformanceMax&utm_content=&network=x&placement=&target=&matchtype=&utm_campaign=16929735023&ad_type=responsive_pmax&adposition=&kwd_id=&gad_source=5&gclid=EAIaIQobChMIp7nzhZi-hwMVN5RQBh1DPAuYEAAYBCAAEgLPn_D_BwE

LaBianca, J. (2023, December 13). *10 Inspiring Stories of Extreme Forgiveness That Will Lift Your Spirits.* Reader's Digest.

https://www.rd.com/list/inspiring-forgiveness-stories/

McCoy, K. (2020, June 23) *The Healing Power of Forgiveness.* Psychology Today,

https://www.psychologytoday.com/gb/blog/complicated-love/202006/the-healing-power-forgiveness

McGough, NB. (2024, April 30). *75 Quotes About Forgiveness To Help You Move On.* Southern Living.

https://www.southernliving.com/culture/forgiveness-quotes

Monahan, J B. (2018, May 7). *How to Move on After Being Hurt: Do You Have the Courage to Forgive?* Medium.com.

https://medium.com/@jennifermonahan_28426/do-you-have-the-courage-to-forgive-a42c1dc9f56f

Mosunic, C. *How to Forgive and Let Go: 8 Ways to Practice Forgiveness.* Calm.com

https://www.calm.com/blog/forgive-and-let-go

Platske, LM. (2024, March 4) *Forgive in Difficult Times.*

https://www.upsidethinking.com/the-courage-to-forgive-in-difficult-times

The Courage to Forgive. (2012, November 17)

https://blog.peoplefirstps.com/connect2lead/the-courage-to-forgive

What is Forgiveness? Greater Good Magazine.

https://greatergood.berkeley.edu/topic/forgiveness/definition

Wygant, E. (2023, September 20) *The Transformative Power of Forgiveness: Journey to Healing and Empowerment.*

https://www.linkedin.com/pulse/transformative-power-forgiveness-my-journey-healing-wygant/

Chapter 9

Cultivating Courage in Childhood

—————— ✿✿ ——————

"It's not about being fearless, it's about acting in spite of fear."
~ Veronica Roth

There are many people out there I consider to be fearless, but let's stop for a moment and think about what that truly means. Sometimes, people are described as being "fearless" when that's not really the case. As Veronica Roth suggests, people are not necessarily fearless—what I mean by this is that the fear is still there (it hasn't disappeared). The notion of being fearless is not about feeling fearless as such; it's about taking action regardless of the fear you feel. People who appear fearless often take action and work through the fear. They're described as being "fearless" because they don't let fear stop them. To do this, they need courage. It's the key ingredient.

The experiences we have as a child play a crucial role in shaping who we become when we're adults. If we feel confident from a young age, we have the potential to blossom and feel empowered, so as we get older, we're not afraid to face challenges head-on. Of course, we face those things with determination and resilience. I personally recognize the importance of courage in childhood, and I believe that courageous fire isn't solely applicable in adults; it can be cultivated during our childhood years. You see, courage influences us throughout our lives.

While I want to encourage courageous fire in leadership, I believe this can be cultivated and nurtured from a young age. As an educator, I know that several of the students in our school systems will one day be the leaders of tomorrow, and I want them to embrace their courageous fire.

In this chapter, we'll reflect on our childhood experiences and consider how they have influenced and impacted our development or choices in life. We'll also think about the role of confidence and how this instills bravery in children and how our courage equips us with the tools we need to navigate challenges confidently. We'll also explore some practical strategies and review the role that parents, educators, and mentors play in encouraging and nurturing courage.

There's a connection between childhood courage and lifelong leadership that we'll uncover in this chapter. It's the foundation of your courageous fire, but it fuels the decisions and actions you take as a leader.

Let's talk more about cultivating courage in childhood, starting with your own childhood experiences.

Your Childhood Experiences

There's no doubt that your experiences during childhood shape your behaviors, values, and the type of person you become as an adult. If we take time to reflect on our own childhood, we can gain valuable insights and learn valuable lessons. They can guide us in cultivating courage, both in ourselves and in the children we mentor. As a leader who is passionate about education and who has worked in the sector for decades, cultivating courage in children (and the staff in my charge) is extremely important to me. They are the future.

I'm a firm believer that if we want to cultivate courage in others, we have to model it ourselves first. It's that idea of leading by example, and when we take bold and courageous action, we're inspiring others—and they look up to us. When others, especially children, see us stepping out of our comfort zone, tackling challenges head-on, and showing resilience when things don't go our way, they learn from us. Again, in similar words to the Roth quote presented at the beginning of this chapter: Bravery doesn't mean we're not afraid, but it does mean we can move forward despite it.

Courage is refusing to stand still or move backward.

We all have some positive and negative experiences as children—regardless, they're our experiences, and we learn from them. They shape who we are today. The lessons learned, the challenges faced, and the support received during our younger years create the foundation for our emotional and psychological development. Positive experiences, such as encouragement from parents or mentors, foster confidence and a sense of self-worth, while overcoming adversity can build resilience and determination. Having such influences at an early age helps mold our character and set the stage for how we handle stress, pursue our goals, and approach relationships in the future. The negative experiences still teach us; for instance, if we face a setback or something doesn't turn out as planned, we learn how to move past those things and develop. I like to think of every experience as one of life's lessons.

All of our experiences serve as a blueprint for our leadership style, too. For instance, a person who grew up in an environment that encouraged curiosity and learning is likely to value and promote continuous improvement and innovation within their team. In contrast, those who've experienced empathy and inclusiveness are more likely to lead with compassion and a focus on creating a supportive, collaborative work culture. If we reflect on our own experiences, we can gain a deeper understanding of our inherent strengths and areas for growth. This allows us to leverage our past to become more effective and courageous leaders. Personally, I've had several strong and determined role models in my life, and for that, I am extremely fortunate. They've certainly shaped the person and leader I've become today.

When reflecting on significant moments or people in your life that have left a lasting impression on you, it's important to remember the positive and negative experiences, as mentioned earlier. Whether we like it or not, they both make an impact. When we reflect on the past, there's always a lesson to learn that makes us who we are. For each moment and person, you should consider what you've learned and what your experiences teach you about courage and bravery. You can connect those experiences to who you are today and then allow those insights to guide you as you move forward.

For instance, someone who had financial hardships and limited access to resources throughout their childhood, yet whose parents worked hard and encouraged them to pursue education, likely has similar values instilled from a young age. They'll most likely be resilient, able to persevere through tough times, and willing to take on challenges while inspiring those around them to do this, too. That's because modeling courage inspires others to be courageous as well.

Yes, the components of courage can be contagious!

Walking through the Fear as a Child

When I think back on my childhood, I often reflect on today's youth and the experiences they have or don't have and how their experiences shape a strong sense of self and courage.

My father, a Jehovah's Witness, instilled a lot of responsibility in us from a young age. We had to present to the congregation, follow an outline, and create our content. In fact, there were many activities we were responsible for, but the biggest challenge was going out into "field service." This involved going door to door to share the word of Jehovah, information about Bible study, or simply talking to people in the local community. We also stood in public places to share the same message.

As a child, I found these experiences daunting, and my older brother absolutely hated it. Not everyone liked, shared, or even wanted to hear our views. It was embarrassing for both of us, but it was a responsibility and expectation from our father. These experiences taught me a lot about how people perceive others, how anyone (including your peers) can make fun of you for doing something different, and how this can close your mind to experiences you might not like but can learn from. While it didn't bother me as much, it really mortified my older brother. But in those days, you didn't argue; you just did as you were told.

Between the ages of five and thirteen, I was consistently engaged in these activities. As I got older, the frequency decreased, but it was daunting because you never knew what response you'd get from the people you encountered. I was walking through my fear, wondering what others would say, think, or feel about me for doing what I was expected to do. Today, I realize that while it's important to be aware of others' perceptions, I don't need to own or carry the perceptions of others because they aren't mine to bear. Following through with expectations and responsibilities, despite others' opinions, helped me to develop that courage and strength from a very young age.

My father's unwavering expectations, whether he knew it or not, fostered a sense of courage that eventually ignited the courageous fire within me. His approach, from a different generation, simply told us, "This is the expectation; this is what you will do." There was no room for fighting back then, and that sense of courage became deeply ingrained in me, shaping the courageous fire that I carry today.

Reflection Time

Before you move on, I want you to think about where your own courage comes from. Take some time to reflect on your past experiences, and specifically reflect on the times you've been brave or have been encouraged by someone else to be brave. You could also reflect on times when you've encouraged or recognized the courageous actions of others.

Then, follow the steps below:

- Think about the situation. How did this impact you or the other person? Do you think this experience had an impact?

- Now, consider the outcome. What happened as a result of this? Did it lead to any changes or developments? What did you learn?

- Finally, consider the future. How can you use what you learned from this experience when moving forward?

When you understand how your own experiences have impacted your courage (and life as a whole), it's easier to see how you can encourage courage in future generations.

It's a good idea to log your reflections and thoughts in a journal so you can go back and reflect again in the future. You can also encourage the children you mentor to do the same, as this can help ensure personal growth and development and cultivate courage.

So now we've talked about your courage; let's talk about how you can nurture courage in children.

Nurturing Courage in Children from a Young Age

There are so many benefits of nurturing courage in children from a young age. There's no doubt that it has a positive impact on their life, and even when they're facing difficulties, courage gives them the tools they need to rise to the challenge.

The benefits of nurturing courage are that:

- It ensures a child feels happy and fulfilled.

- It helps to improve a child's confidence.

- It encourages them to take the initiative and act independently.

- It helps them to make better decisions.

- It helps them to achieve more. This could include personal development or academic success.

- It increases the empathy a child feels for others.

- It improves communication skills and helps to build stronger relationships.

- It can improve how they handle stress and manage anxiety.

- It helps them bounce back when things don't go their way (yes, resilience).

Being courageous is empowering. It keeps us motivated and determined as we strive toward our goals (or dreams). It helps people develop and grow and shapes their future. For children, this is particularly important as they are still learning and developing. It allows them to develop a more positive mindset, as they know from an early age that it's okay to fail as long as you keep learning as you move forward. Being able to accept and learn from failure is an invaluable skill.

To nurture courage in children, several strategies can be employed. This includes offering support, modeling courageous behavior, and helping them to develop their emotional intelligence. When praising children, you should always emphasize the effort they invest rather than solely focusing on their achievements. This approach encourages persistence and resilience and acknowledges that setbacks are valuable learning opportunities. Encouraging children to explore new activities and step beyond their comfort zone by taking calculated risks is essential when nurturing courage. Introducing a child to new sports or hobbies is an effective way to begin this journey of growth and self-discovery. Teaching problem-solving skills also equips children to navigate the challenges they face and encourages critical thinking skills, helping them deal with difficult situations better.

Sometimes, the most courageous thing we can do is embrace our mistakes. We all make them, and owning them shows integrity. I always remember that a child of a friend of mine got into trouble with his teacher because the teacher gave an incorrect answer, and he put his hand up and corrected her—not in a disrespectful way, but more inquisitively because he was confused by the teacher's answer. The teacher didn't take this well, and after reprimanding him, she complained to his parents about his behavior, leaving them slightly bewildered when she said that he'd embarrassed her in front of the class. The child protested that it wasn't his intention.

It got me thinking that, surely, it's more important to teach the correct things than it is to worry about the embarrassment of getting it wrong. While I understand how she felt, as long as it was done respectfully, the child displayed bravery, which, in my eyes, we should be nurturing. Instead, the child was punished for being courageous. The truth is, no one is perfect, and this could have been such a different learning experience if the teacher had simply embraced the comment and acknowledged the mistake. By doing so, the teacher would've shown courage, and it would have made her so much more relatable to the other students.

It's this notion that we have to be perfect that holds us back, and by trying to silence confident kids, we're essentially holding them back, too. This is not the type of culture I want to embrace in the schools I work in. Being able to make mistakes and own up to them shows confidence, and it proves that we're human. This is a huge part of being courageous. We can learn so much more by owning our mistakes, and by doing this, we set ourselves apart as a role model by displaying honesty and integrity, acknowledging that we all make mistakes, learning from the mistakes we make, and showing resilience by overcoming the situation and moving forward.

We should never make a child or young person (or anyone else for that matter) feel like they have done wrong by speaking up respectfully, as this can have negative consequences, especially for children. They may not feel confident enough to speak up or ask questions in the future, so this experience could hinder their learning. We need to learn from examples like this, and as adults, we need to lead the way and acknowledge that we do make mistakes, and that's okay. This sets a good example for the children we are a role model to and gets us ready to discuss the role parents, educators, and mentors play in fostering and nurturing courage.

What Role Do Parents, Educators, and Mentors Play in Fostering Courage?

It shouldn't come as a surprise to point out that parents, educators, and mentors play a key role in nurturing and cultivating courage in children. Parents are their primary caregivers and role models, and their behavior, attitudes, and beliefs ultimately influence the child throughout their life. Educators and mentors can play an important part, too, as they spend a lot of time with the child.

Let's look at these in turn and discuss the role each plays in fostering courage in children and young people.

Parents

Having parents who encourage us to be courageous can empower us as children. Our parents or main caregivers are our first role models in life, and they can help to set us up for success. We've already discussed some ways to foster courage in kids, and for parents, this is similar. Parents should model courageous behavior and provide emotional support to their children so that they feel safe and are, therefore, able to talk about any fears and anxieties they have. As a parent, you need to be able to listen and show empathy. If children have a safe and supportive environment, they'll feel so much more confident, which will help them become more independent when making decisions. I've said this already, but a parent should always look to praise effort rather than success, as this helps to alter a child's mindset so they can keep going, even if they've faced setbacks.

Educators

I'm sure that most of us can reflect on some teachers or educators who have influenced us or impacted our lives. Educators are often a huge part of a child's life, which is why they also have a role to play in fostering courage. Again, it's about providing a safe environment that makes students feel able to ask questions, express their thoughts, and make mistakes that they can learn from. Educators are good at identifying strengths and nurturing this can give students the courage to pursue their goals and passions. They can achieve anything they set their mind to—it's time to embed this idea from a young age!

Again, an educator can help to build confidence in children, and one way to do that is by providing them with leadership opportunities. For instance, allowing students to lead group projects, discussions, or activities at school encourages them to take on responsibility. All of these experiences encourage growth and make space for children to be courageous.

Mentors

I've had several mentors in my life who have provided me with invaluable guidance and support by drawing from their own experiences. They can make a huge difference and certainly have a role to play in nurturing and cultivating courage.

A mentor offers reliable and consistent support that helps to keep others motivated. They should inspire others by sharing their courageous stories of how they overcame challenges and faced their fears. They can also offer constructive feedback that points out areas for growth and improvement and guides others on how to develop. Mentors can also help people set realistic and achievable goals as they set a clear path and use their courage to take steps toward achieving the things they want.

The efforts of parents, educators, and mentors are instrumental in cultivating courage in children and young people. These key figures can create a nurturing environment where kids can act courageously, overcome challenges, and build both resilience and confidence.

Our experiences in childhood play a pivotal role in shaping our courage later in our lives. Throughout our childhood years, we are incredibly receptive to learning, so if we're exposed to positive examples of courageous behavior, it starts to reflect in our actions and attitudes. Having positive role models throughout our lives lays the foundations of courage and its development. This is why we can reflect on our own experiences now and consider what impact they've had on us in relation to the courage we have. Some of us will have gone through life with very little courage, and maybe courage is something we're working on right now. That's fine. It took me a long time to fully understand the pivotal role that courage plays in our lives, so until we have that realization, improving our courage isn't something we necessarily work on improving. But my point is, if you have or are working on your courage, it's a skill you should start cultivating in the younger generations early on so they can lead a more courageous life!

We want our young people to be independent, determined, resilient, and able to overcome obstacles of their own. We want them to stand up for what they believe in and pursue their goals, regardless of the difficulties they face. But if we truly want this, we need to cultivate their courage today.

Everything we've covered in this chapter links back to the concept of courageous fire in leadership. Courageous fire isn't just a quality that emerges in adulthood; it's something that we can develop as we grow. Having supportive environments and positive role models, being encouraged to take risks, and learning from mistakes all help shape our future courageous leaders. A person who has been nurtured with courage from a young age tends to be a much more empathetic, resilient, and determined leader throughout their lives.

We should encourage others to nurture their courage, just like us. Let's use our courageous fire for the greater good—to breed more courage in others. As we head into the next chapter, it's time to take our courageous fire to the next level. We'll be talking about using your courageous fire in your everyday life.

Let's embrace courageous fire to do great things beyond leading and use it in our everyday lives.

References

5 Steps to Cultivate Courage and Confidence. Blue Osa.

https://www.blueosa.com/5-things-you-can-do-to-cultivate-courage/?utm_term=&utm_campaign=&utm_source=google&utm_medium=cpc&hsa_acc=7178588013&hsa_cam=20927664681&hsa_grp=&hsa_ad=&hsa_src=x&hsa_tgt=&hsa_kw=&hsa_mt=&hsa_net=adwords&hsa_ver=3&gad_source=5&gclid=EAIaIQobChMI4qqogq--hwMVXZRQBh1JLCxGEAAYAyAAEgJUH_D_BwE

Building Courage in Children: A Key to Future Success. (2024, March 7).

https://balancedmartialarts.com/2024/03/07/building-courage-in-children-a-key-to-future-success/

Carlyle, R. (2022, March 5) *How to Help Build Resilience in Your Child.* The Times.

https://www.thetimes.com/life-style/health-fitness/article/how-to-help-build-resilience-in-your-child-qrwc2rdlr?id=17515457033&gad_source=5&gclid=EAIaIQobChMIzPfq3ay-hwMVa6NQBh2jZSdGEAAYASAAEgIRH_D_BwE

Cavanagh, SR. (2023) *How to Support Kids to be Brave.*

https://psyche.co/guides/how-to-support-kids-to-be-brave-and-face-difficult-challenges

Clare, V. (2021, February 1) *What Our Children Can Teach Us About Courage.* Medium.com

https://medium.com/family-matters-2/what-our-children-can-teach-us-about-courage-cd2b2396d6d0

Courage Activities and Lessons for the Classroom. (2019, April 25). Tarheelstate.

https://www.tarheelstateteacher.com/blog/teaching-courage-in-classroom

Gillett, R. (2016, November 26). *30 Scientific Ways Your Childhood Affects Your Success as an Adult*. Business Insider.

https://www.businessinsider.com/how-your-childhood-affects-your-success-as-an-adult-2016-11?r=US&IR=T

How to Be Brave: Understanding and Overcoming Fear. (2024, April 18) Better Help.

https://www.betterhelp.com/advice/how-to/how-to-be-brave-and-overcome-fear/?utm_source=AdWords&utm_medium=Search_PPC_c&utm_term=PerformanceMax&utm_content=&network=x&placement=&target=&matchtype=&utm_campaign=16929735023&ad_type=responsive_pmax&adposition=&kwd_id=&gad_source=5&gclid=EAIaIQobChMIu4qGh62-hwMVCYlQBh2Q1i8qEAAYAiAAEgJRO_D_BwE

How to Teach Courage to Children. (2024, February 22). That Character Corner.

https://www.thecharactercorner.com/how-to-teach-courage-to-children/

Khong, S. (2021, November 11). *Impact of Mentoring on Youth: Why Every Kid Needs a Mentor*.

https://www.bgca.org/news-stories/2021/November/impact-of-mentoring-on-youth-why-every-kid-needs-a-mentor/

Kids and Courage: Courage in Everyday Life. The Center for Parenting Education.

https://centerforparentingeducation.org/library-of-articles/self-esteem/kids-and-courage/

Kozlowski, T. (2022, September 20) *How to Better Nurture Yourself and Why It's Essential For A Balanced Life.*

https://www.linkedin.com/pulse/how-better-nurture-yourself-why-its-essential-life-terri-kozlowski/

Mathukutty, P V. (2023, July 28). *Nurturing Courage in Children: Importance and Benefits.* Simply Life Tips.

https://simplylifetips.com/nurturing-courage-in-children-benefits/#:~:text=Cultivating%20courage%20in%20children%20is%20a%20transformative%20gift,the%20confidence%20and%20resilience%20they%20need%20to%20thrive

Naik, A. (2023, November 20) *How to Teach Courage and Bravery in Kids.*

https://www.gohenry.com/uk/blog/family/courage-and-bravery-to-kids

Redgrave-Hogg, S. (2023, September 19) *Building Courage in Kids: 4 Ways to be Brave.*

https://happiful.com/building-courage-in-kids-4-ways-to-be-brave

Rich, J D. (2017, October 23). *Courageous Parents, Smart Kids.* Psychology Today.

https://www.psychologytoday.com/us/blog/parenting-purpose/201710/courageous-parents-smart-kids

Shenfield, T. *How to Help Your Child Develop.* Psy-Ed.

https://www.psy-ed.com/wpblog/child-courage/

Smith, C L. *How to Teach Courage to Young Children.* Momentsaday.com

https://www.momentsaday.com/how-to-teach-courage-to-young-children/

The 50 Best Courage Quotes for Kids to Inspire Bravery. Suchalittlewhile.com

https://www.suchalittlewhile.com/best-courage-quotes-for-kids/

Waldman, M. (2022, April 6). *Bravery in Our Children Instilling Values and Self-Awareness.*

https://myfeellinks.com/blogs/news/bravery-in-our-children-instilling-values-and-self-awareness

Young, K. *Building Courage in Kids – How to Teach Kids to Be Brave.* Hey Sigmund.

https://www.heysigmund.com/building-courage-in-kids/#:~:text=How%20to%20Build%20Courage%20in%20Kids.%201%20Speak,them%20how%20to%20use%20it.%20...%20More%20items

Chapter 10

Courageous Fire in Everyday Life

———— ❈ ————

You've made it to the final chapter, and it's time to talk about ways to use your courageous fire in your everyday life. Here, we'll be exploring courage at its core and how it can impact your daily experiences.

"Inaction breeds doubt and fear. Action breeds confidence and courage. If you want to conquer fear, do not sit home and think about it. Go out and get busy." ~ Dale Carnegie

Courage is not merely an occasional act but a habit of bravery and resilience during difficult times—those in which we face many challenges. Your courage manifests in moments that are both small and significant, as it helps shape your response to adversity and guides your decision-making. It's up to you to act upon that response because, as the quote suggests, conquerors do not do nothing; they are action-takers.

As we make our way through the final chapter, we'll be exploring ways to help you become an action-taker. This means incorporating your courage into your everyday routines, interactions, and all-important decision-making processes. Whether you're navigating uncertain times or embracing the opportunities that present themselves to you, your courage can empower you to lead a more fulfilling and impactful life in everything you do.

This is why it's so important to cultivate your courage and embrace it early on so you become habitually courageous. It's time to own your courageous fire and use it to propel yourself forward as you inspire those around you and foster a deeper sense of personal fulfillment.

Let's begin with one simple question. . . .

Have You Ignited Your Courageous Fire?

Before you answer this question, I want you to pause for a moment and reflect on your relationship with courage.

- *What does that look like?*

- Maybe you've even started to integrate strategies and insights you've taken from earlier chapters, but do you feel the fire of courage roaring?

- *Are you using your courage in your everyday life?*

The reason I'm asking you this, and by now you may already understand, is that courageous fire is not merely a concept but a lived experience and a proactive approach to facing challenges with resilience and conviction.

Think back to those moments you recall in which you've summoned your courage. Maybe you were taking a risk, navigating a difficult conversation, or even standing up for something you believe in. Whatever instance springs to your mind, it's illuminated by the sparks of the courageous fire within you. It's demonstrating your ability to jump over the highest and longest barriers while inspiring other people along the way. That's because your courageous fire is showing you just how capable you are. It's telling you that *you can do it* because you can achieve whatever you want to accomplish if you put your mind (and courageous fire) to it.

Now, I know the sparks that light your courageous fire are there, and you probably know this too, even if they're not igniting as quickly as you'd hoped. This chapter will help you nurture and expand your inner flame, and soon, we'll be discussing practical ways to incorporate your fire into everyday situations. We'll be focusing on how it can empower you and help you cultivate a mindset that embraces transformation and growth.

You'll soon learn how to spark the flame yourself and in those around you!

Reflection Time

Let's pause and reflect on how you're incorporating courage into your life. Draw on the insights and strategies you've gathered so far, and consider those moments of courage we talked about in the previous section.

Take a moment to think. . . .

How has your perception of courage changed?

Are you more willing to step outside of your comfort zone?

Even if you feel fear, are you still able to engage in difficult conversations and take bold actions?

Now, think back to some of the practices discussed in the earlier chapters of this book and consider your biggest takeaways. *Which strategies are you embracing? Which are you finding the most challenging?*

Use this opportunity to celebrate your progress so far—you deserve it!

Also, identify areas for development and growth. Developing and growing your courageous fire is an ongoing process. It's a continuous learning curve that requires adaptations and tweaks.

If you acknowledge your wins as well as the challenges you're facing, you're nurturing the fire within and paving the way for greater fulfillment in the future.

Eleven Easy Ways to Incorporate Courage into Your Daily Lives

I want you to think of courage as a muscle that you must stretch, flex, and exercise to help it get stronger. I get it—the stretching and flexing part isn't always easy, but there are some steps you can take to make this easier so you can incorporate courage into your daily life.

I want your courage to become a positive habit that you automatically embrace, especially when feeling moments of fear, hesitation, or self-doubt. Those feelings are trying to control you, and they have to stop. Your courage should kick in here and help you push past those feelings with ease.

There are eleven simple ways to incorporate courage into your daily life:

1. Own your courage.

    What I mean by this is being content with being yourself and using your courage to be proud of being you. Don't be afraid to share your flaws, show vulnerabilities, and allow others to see your imperfections. It's about authenticity, so allow yourself to shine in your own way, doing your own thing unapologetically.

2. Be accountable and responsible.

    Being accountable means holding yourself to account, so when you say you'll do something, you motivate and remind yourself to do it. You're responsible for your life and the choices you make, so if you don't like something, you have the power to change it. Being responsible and accountable offers us a sense of freedom.

3. Don't be afraid to say no and speak up.

    Sometimes, we must teach ourselves how to say "no." So many people feel obliged to say "yes"—often because it feels like it's the polite thing to do. But saying "yes" all the time doesn't always serve you, and it allows others to take advantage of you. Saying "no" takes courage. It shows you're not willing to let anyone take advantage of you—so does speaking up, so don't be afraid to share your opinions if you witness an injustice, especially if you feel strongly about it.

4.   Listen to others.

You should always listen to others—and this means people who you think are wrong, who disagree with you—when you want to give advice or when people are asking you for advice, and always be sure to thank others for sharing their views. It takes courage to listen to others when you aren't on the same page or if it's not what you want to hear, but sometimes it's valuable or necessary.

5.   Keep learning and growing.

To cultivate your courage, it's important to continuously learn and grow. Sometimes, you've got to learn something new, try doing things a different way, and step into the unknown from time to time. It takes courage to seize such opportunities because we don't always get things right the first time we try them—but that's okay. Having the courage to learn encourages growth and, with it, new opportunities.

6.   Practice being grateful.

If I asked you to reflect on three things you're grateful for today, what would you say? Would you know instantly, or do you need time to think about it? Sometimes, we take the things we already have for granted, but reminding ourselves and feeling thankful for what we have can change our whole mindset for the better. Remember to thank people and focus on the things you feel grateful for. Gratitude should be shared.

7. Choose to be happy.

Of course, there are things that make us unhappy at times, but sometimes, it's a choice. It's down to you to decide to be kind to others, to think happy thoughts, and to spend time doing things that bring you joy. You can choose whether you look on the bright side or not, but having a good attitude that focuses on positive things is a courageous act. Regardless of what's happening, you're focused on your goals, and nothing will stand in your way.

8. Help people.

Courage is often about leading the way and setting a positive example to others. It takes courage to help someone, especially if they don't tend to help others; however, helping those people sets a good example of the way things should be. We shouldn't help others because we expect them to help us—we should do it because it's the right thing (morally) to do. Helping someone who can't pay you back but needs help also shows empathy. The act of helping says a lot about you and the type of person you are.

9. If you're in the wrong, apologize.

Saying you're sorry goes a long way because it's a bold action. It takes courage to hold your hands up and admit you're wrong or made a mistake because it takes us out of our comfort zone. Nobody really likes to be in the wrong, but we all are sometimes. Courage means stepping out of your comfort zone regularly, acknowledging your own behavior, and owning your mistakes. Acting this way has the power to enhance relationships and heal any rifts.

10. Appreciate the small things.

Life doesn't have to be about the big events and material things. Although those things can be nice, you should first make time to enjoy the small things, such as a stroll at sunrise, a walk in the forest or by the beach, the taste of your favorite food or drink, and even laughter. It takes courage to say, "I don't care about what other people have because I'm staying in my own lane and doing my own thing." The small stuff counts, so appreciate and embrace it—just take time to enjoy it.

11. Embrace self-love.

I've seen it so many times when people are unhappy with themselves. Self-love is a powerful thing, but it's also a courageous act. It's okay to have imperfections, be your own best friend, and be compassionate about yourself. It's easy to pick fault with ourselves, but recognizing our worth isn't that simple—it's a courageous act and maybe even the most important act of all because it helps us build our confidence and enhance our mindset. Feeling good about yourself can have such a positive impact, and it can inspire others.

12. Use your mistakes as a learning curve.

I've already mentioned that holding your hands up and admitting you've done wrong is a courageous act, but to extend this further, you have the power to turn this into a positive by learning from that mistake. Take some time to reflect on what went wrong and what you should have done differently. Be compassionate with yourself and make a conscious choice to move forward and grow. Never give up!

These are just simple ways to start embracing courage as part of your everyday life. If you practice courageousness, you're ensuring that every day is a courageous day. Your fire will roar as this becomes more prominent, and you'll grow your courage with confidence.

Daily courageous acts are the fuel to your courageous fire.

(It's More Than Just) a Scooter Story

As I reflect on the journey we've taken through this book—from the activities, reflection, strategies, stories, and principles—I can't help but think about a man (or big brother) I met when I was seventeen years old. It was my first year of college at California State University, Long Beach (CSULB). I was far away from home with no family or friends around, and I was probably a little naïve to life external to my hometown community. I lived in the dorms, and my world was suddenly much larger than the San Francisco community I had grown up in. There I was, in 1989, and lucky enough to meet a guy, Jackson, unbeknown to me, would enhance my mindset. He was a few years older than me and had a scholarship to play sports at Long Beach State.

Now, let's rewind just a little to a time prior to us all attending CSULB. I was aware that Jackson had been through challenging times, just as I had, living and growing up in a challenging environment. These challenges led to the creation of perseverance, grit, and a can-do attitude in a human being.

Now, it's worth making it known that Jackson did go on to play professional sports for a few teams. But in 1989, Jackson lived in the same dorms as I did and shared a room with another big brother mentor I got to know.

In this new space without relatives or parents, Jackson and others in the college community showed me compassion, grace, gratitude, and oversight. I'll always be thankful for that, but there's a story that sticks in my mind. . . .

I vividly remember my scooter story. You see, I had some money from my student loans and wanted to buy a scooter to get around campus and the community. Jackson and a few others accompanied me to buy it. Just as we were about to meet the person selling the scooter, Jackson asked how much money I had. When I told him, he asked me to give it to him. I asked why but didn't really get an answer. He insisted, and I trusted him, so reluctantly, I handed it over. He took some of it, put it in his pocket, and handed the rest back to me, instructing me to tell the seller that this was all I had.

I didn't realize it at the time, but Jackson was teaching me how to negotiate and barter, protecting me in a way I hadn't expected. In the end, I bought the scooter, and don't worry, Jackson was an honorable guy, so he returned the remaining money to me afterward.

From that moment, I realized Jackson was someone who would protect me. He displayed courage in everyday life. His history of courage, exemplified by surviving challenges, was evident. It was something he showed without even trying—to him, acting courageously was a habit.

I share this story about Jackson because he exhibits courage in everyday life. He looked out for me when I was in college, guiding me and showing me the way. Courageous fire today embodies my ability to facilitate difficult conversations, provide opportunities for others to speak their truth, and practice courage regularly.

I've been extremely fortunate. The mentors and people who have influenced my life have seen certain things in me, and I've learned from them to develop the skill to show courage in every way, shape, and manner on a regular basis.

Courage is a guiding principle in my life. I own my courage. I'm responsible for the courage, and I am accountable to be courageous. But you can only provide that if you listen, learn, grow, and practice courage.

All of these things are at the core of courageous fire!

Will you make courage a guiding principle in your life?

How to Embrace Courage as a Guiding Principle

We all have philosophies and beliefs that we live by, and in this section, we're going to talk about how courage can become your guiding principle. Courage is there for you during the good times and the bad, and all you have to do is be open to it.

Now, we've already talked through some ways of incorporating courage into your life, but embracing courage as a guiding principle alters how you approach challenges, make decisions, and embrace opportunities.

Courage isn't a simple case of facing your fears, although that's a huge part of it. It's about using it to drive forward, lead with integrity, and pursue your passions. I want you to achieve your goals and aspirations, which is why I'll talk you through some ways that will allow you to use your courage as a guiding principle and ensure it's embedded in everything you do.

- Begin by understanding your purpose and core values. When you're clear about what matters to you, acting courageously becomes easier because it means acting in alignment with those values. Make sure you know what drives you, what you want to achieve, and what beliefs shape or influence your decision-making.

- Practice self-awareness so that you recognize moments when you're being held back by self-doubt or fear. If you're aware of those feelings, you can then take action—confront them head-on by acknowledging those fears, but don't allow them to influence your actions. They're signaling to you that it's time to push beyond your comfort zone.

- Don't wait for big moments or grand gestures. Just take small steps because it's often those small, consistent steps that build true bravery. You can do this by setting small, achievable goals (of course, it should be challenging, as all goals should be). As you accomplish each of your goals, your courage will grow, and over time, you'll become confident when tackling bigger challenges.

- Surround yourself with people who support and inspire you to act in a courageous way. There's no doubt that our mentors, loved ones, and peers can provide valuable encouragement (sometimes giving us a push when needed) and perspective. I was lucky enough to have an excellent support network of reliable people. I learned from them and drew strength from their courage. You're not alone, so you don't have to face every challenge without support.

- Ensure your courage aligns with your integrity. Integrity is a huge part of being courageous because those courageous actions should reflect your true self, as well as your moral and ethical standards. Your integrity strengthens the relationships you have because it builds trust with others and strengthens your sense of purpose and fulfillment.

If you make courage a guiding principle, you're empowering yourself to lead a life of authenticity, purpose, and fulfillment. Your courage will help you navigate life and all its complexities. It will also help you make bold decisions as you keep moving toward your life aspirations. Just remember that regardless of how small your courageous act is, it still contributes to the development of your courageous fire. It's giving you a gentle and encouraging push toward the life you desire and will help you become the leader that you want to be.

Own Your Courageous Fire

It's time. Time to own your courageous fire. It's about stepping out and facing adversity with a sense of confidence and fearlessness that saturates every aspect of your life. To own your courageous fire, you must deeply connect with yourself and others, driven by an inner strength that guides your actions and decisions. Your courageous fire is at the core of your ability to live with purpose and authenticity.

If you feel the urge to stand up for what you believe in, lead with integrity, and face your fears, it's the inner flame of your courageous fire driving you. Once lit, it creates a powerful connection to yourself and with those around you. It's encouraging you to step into a space of assuredness, and it's a powerful but quiet recognition of your own capabilities and self-worth.

Your courage allows you to take on the challenges you face with calm determination. It knows that you have the strength to navigate anything that comes your way and encourages those around you to find and embrace their inner flame, too.

You have already learned many of the skills you need to own your courageous fire, but there are three principles you can follow to ensure this. You should:

- Show compassion – Be kind to others and especially to yourself. Understand that mistakes and setbacks are part of your life, but this allows you to bounce back more determined and stronger than before.

- Stay true to your values – Your values are the foundation of your courageous fire, so it's important to stay true to your beliefs, even if that's difficult. Keep your inner fire strong without faltering to reinforce your sense of purpose and direction.

- Lead by example and inspire others – Demonstrate your courageous fire and what that means by allowing your actions to inspire the people around you. Lead with confidence and integrity so that others find the courage to do the same.

You'll find that owning your courageous fire allows you to live your life in an authentic and purposeful way. It makes you more resilient and confident, and it will transform your life for the better.

It's important that you see your courageous fire as a journey rather than a destination, as it requires continuous nurturing and commitment. As it grows, you can trust your courageousness and allow its flame to light the path and ignite your potential within. It's the driving force that empowers you to live boldly, lead authentically, and leave a lasting impact.

As we close this final chapter, I just want you to take a moment to reflect on the core principles of your courageous fire and consider how you can use them to transform your relationships, your leadership, and your life.

Throughout this chapter, we've focused on courage empowering you and how it can act as a guiding principle to help you transform a range of aspects and events in your life. It's also a transformative journey for you on a personal level, and I hope you recognize that this isn't the end but more like the beginning of a lifelong, courageous journey. I know my courageous journey isn't over as I continue to nurture and commit to both self-discovery and growth.

You are capable of more than you realize, but this journey is yours to shape, just like mine is my own, and I say that to you with my courageous fire burning brightly. There's no limit to what you can achieve, and while you've come so far already, I know you want and deserve more.

"Life shrinks or expands in proportion to one's courage." ~ Anaïs Nin

References

Bazzy, R. *Summon Your Courage*. Proctor Gallagher.

https://www.proctorgallagherinstitute.com/42416/summon-your-courage

Castle, T. (2024, June 4) *How to Cultivate Courage in Everyday Life*. Medium.

https://medium.com/@timcastle_/how-to-cultivate-courage-in-everyday-life-c627d3aaa591

Fearless Leadership: How Do You Develop Great Leaders? Transcend Culture.

https://transcendculture.co/fearless-leadership/

Gavin, M. (2020, March 10) *3 Examples of Courageous Leaders & Lessons You Can Learn From Them*.

https://online.hbs.edu/blog/post/courageous-leaders?c1=GAW_CM_NW&source=INTL_CLIMB_PMAX&cr2=content_-_international_-_climb_-_pmax&kw=climb&cr5=&cr6=&cr7=c&utm_campaign=content_-_international_-_climb_-_pmax&utm_term=climb&gad_source=5&gclid=EAIaIQobChMI5JTswrq-hwMVU5JQBh0tqyqiEAAYBCAAEgIwWfD_BwE

How to Develop Your Own Courage and Bravery in the Face of Change. (2023, June 9) Twist Consultant.

https://www.twistconsultants.co.uk/blog/2023/6/9/how-to-develop-your-own-courage-and-bravery-in-the-face-of-change

How to Show Courage in Everyday Life (Step-by-Step). (2023, February 16)

https://leadershiphq.com.au/courage-in-everyday-life/#:~:text=It%20means%2

0facing%20your%20fears,and%20how%20to%20practise%20it.

McDonald, JN. (2023, June 28). *65 Courage Quotes to Motivate and Inspire*. Southern Living.

https://www.southernliving.com/culture/quotes-about-courage

McDonald, S. (2022, October 21). *15 Everyday Acts of Courage*. Linked In.

https://www.linkedin.com/pulse/15-everyday-acts-courage-sonia-mcdonald-dickson-/

Mutiwasekwa, S-L. (2020, June 22). *Stepping Into Your Personal Power*. Psychology Today.

https://www.psychologytoday.com/us/blog/the-upside-things/202006/stepping-your-personal-power

Own Your Courage. Mood Surfing.

https://moodsurfing.com/own-your-courage/

Raim, E. (2018, October 4) *Guts Over Fear: Learning How to Summon Your Courage*. PDXWIT.

https://www.pdxwit.org/blog/2018/10/4/guts-over-fear-learning-how-to-summon-your-courage

Robbins, M. (2021, August 11). *How to Build Your Courage to Achieve Anything*. Success.com

https://www.success.com/how-to-build-your-courage-to-achieve-anything/

Soukup, R. *The Seven Principles of Courage*.

https://ruthsoukup.com/the-seven-principles-of-courage/

Stricklin, C. (2019, August 26) *13 Guiding Principles for Courageous Conversations*. Forbes.

https://www.forbes.com/sites/forbescoachescouncil/2019/08/26/13-guiding-principles-for-courageous-conversations/

Swoboda, K. (2018, October 10) *How to Live a More Courageous Life*.

https://greatergood.berkeley.edu/article/item/how_to_live_a_more_co urageous_life

Top 10 Best Courage Quotes. Jesuit Resource.

https://www.xavier.edu/jesuitresource/online-resources/quote-archive1/courage-quotes#:~:text=%22Each%20time%20we%20face%20our,and%20confidence%20in%20the%20doing.%22&text=%22So%20do%20not%20fear%2C%20for,for%20I%20am%20your%20God.%22&text=%22He%20who%20is%20not%20courageous,will%20accomplish%20nothing%20in%20life.%22&text=%22We%20may%20encounter%20many%20defeats,we%20must%20not%20be%20defeated.%22

Trichel, D. *10 Thinks That Require Courage*. Focus3.

https://focus3.com/10-things-that-require-courage/

Warrell, M. *Find Your Courage*. SuccessConsciousness.

https://www.successconsciousness.com/blog/personal-development/acts-of-courage/

Conclusion

"The mind is not a vessel to be filled, but a fire to be kindled." ~ Plutarch

I wanted to share this quote with you as this book draws to a close. As it suggests, our minds do not exist to be filled with facts and information but to be kindled with curiosity and creativity. That way, you can take over and make decisions about what comes next. You've already been provided with the kindling, so now it's up to you to put into practice what you've learned. Courage is a continuous journey, just like education. So, embrace learning as a journey of discovery, and let your passion for knowledge ignite your true potential.

As we conclude *Courageous Fire: Courageous and Passionate Leadership*, let's take a moment to consider the key takeaways from the unique and innovative journey we've shared.

Together, we've explored the essence of courageous fire and gained a deeper understanding of its inner strength, which pushes us to lead with authenticity, resilience, and empathy. We explored the idea of courage in its various forms and considered how to find our courageous spark while also reflecting on courageous people throughout the world. Gaining this insight helps us understand courage's role in changing the world.

We've also talked a lot about fear, and I've shared honest personal stories and experiences, as well as the role vulnerability plays in that. A huge part of showing courage includes confronting and overcoming fears, so we've discussed this in detail throughout various chapters, and we've also focused on the importance of courage when navigating adversity—something most of us can relate to today, but also something that requires courage. We've also explored resilience, kindness, and compassion and considered how those traits also work in alignment with your courage. There's no doubt that courage is something we must recognize, acknowledge, and utilize, but to do this successfully, we need to be aligned with it and what it stands for.

For me, challenging the status quo chapter was extremely useful as it reminded me of the importance of speaking up to provoke positive change. The status quo is something that needs to be challenged regularly, so it's certainly still relevant (and, at times, eye-opening) as we consider what might've happened should others before us not challenge this.

We've also discussed the importance of courage in relationships and how it is a key component in positive relationships, as well as focusing on ways to communicate and build trust. Whether we have a personal or professional relationship, trust is vital. It was also important to address self-doubt, confidence, and self-belief before moving on to consider courage's role in forgiveness. As I openly explained when reflecting on my own experiences, forgiveness is essential, yet it requires time and patience. As I mentioned, I'm still working through some things in my life that I, too, need to forgive. There's no doubt in my mind that forgiveness takes courage.

As we move to the latter part of the book, I think that reflecting on courage in childhood was a powerful moment for me. My role as a leader in an educational setting really made me reflect on how I foster courage in my workplace and on my own childhood experiences that kindled my courageous fire. The aim of the last chapter was to really get you thinking about putting courageous actions into practice. You had the information, but sometimes, it's the *taking action* part that you may require a little push with.

You've heard the saying that "practice makes perfect," I'm sure, and this is true, but now it's time to make your courageous fire your guiding principle. The importance of courage cannot be overstated. It has the potential to transform lives by enabling us to face challenges head-on, act with integrity, and connect deeply with others. Courage empowers us to take risks, to stand up for what we believe in, and to inspire those around us. It's the foundation of effective leadership and a fulfilling life.

Now, it's time for action. Reflect on the insights and strategies you've gained from this book and apply them to your life. Embrace courage in your decisions, your relationships, and your leadership. Take the first step toward igniting your own courageous fire and let it guide you toward the life you envision.

As you move forward, just remember this. . . .

You have the strength within you to overcome any obstacle, to lead with empathy and conviction, and to inspire others with your courage. Your courageous fire is a powerful force—nurture it, let it grow, and watch it transform your life and the lives of those around you.

And don't forget to believe in yourself, take bold actions, and let your courage shine.

Terrence Davis

www.ingramcontent.com/pod-product-compliance
Lightning Source LLC
Chambersburg PA
CBHW021500180326
41458CB00051B/6898/J